The Supremacy
of God
in Preaching

Part 1: *"The Supremacy of God in Preaching"*
The Harold John Ockenga Lectures on Preaching
Gordon-Conwell Theological Seminary
1988

Part 2: *"Sweet Sovereignty: The Supremacy*
of God in the Preaching of Jonathan Edwards"
The Billy Graham Center Lectures on Preaching
Wheaton College
1984

The Supremacy of God in Preaching

JOHN PIPER

BAKER BOOK HOUSE
Grand Rapids, Michigan 49516

ISBN: 0-8010-7112-7

Eighth printing, September 1997

Printed in the United States of America

Unless otherwise indicated, Scripture references are from the Revised Standard Version (RSV) of the Bible, copyright 1946, 1952, 1971, 1973 by the Division of Christian Education of the National Council of the Churches of Christ in the United States of America.

For information about academic books, resources for Christian leaders, and all new releases available from Baker Book House, visit our web site: http://www.bakerbooks.com/

Library of Congress Cataloging-in-Publication Data

Piper, John, 1946–
    The supremacy of God in preaching / John Piper.
       p.   cm.
    Includes bibliographical references.
    ISBN 0-8010-7112-7
    1. Preaching. 2. Clergy—Religious life. 3. Edwards, Jonathan, 1703–1758—Contributions in preaching. I. Title
BV4211.2P54   1990
251—dc20   90-34898
                                                  CIP

To the people of

Bethlehem Baptist Church

who share the vision of God's supremacy
and live
to savor the vision in worship,
strengthen it in nurture,
and spread it to all the nations
in the name of
Jesus Christ our Lord

Contents

Preface

People are starving for the greatness of God. But most of them would not give this diagnosis of their troubled lives. The majesty of God is an unknown cure. There are far more popular prescriptions on the market, but the benefit of any other remedy is brief and shallow. Preaching that does not have the aroma of God's greatness may entertain for a season, but it will not touch the hidden cry of the soul: "Show me thy glory!"

Years ago during the January prayer week at our church, I decided to preach on the holiness of God from Isaiah 6. I resolved on the first Sunday of the year to unfold the vision of God's holiness found in the first four verses of that chapter:

In the year that king Uzziah died I saw the LORD sitting upon a throne, high and lifted up; and his train filled the temple. Above him stood the seraphim; each had six wings: with two he covered his face, and with two he covered his feet, and with two he flew. And one called to another and said: "Holy, holy, holy is the LORD of hosts; the whole earth is full of his glory." And the foundations of the thresholds shook at the voice of him who called, and the house was filled with smoke.

So I preached on the holiness of God and did my best to display the majesty and glory of such a great and holy God. I gave not one word of application to the lives of the people. Application is essential in the normal course of preaching, but I felt led that day to make a test: Would the passionate portrayal of the greatness of God in and of itself meet the needs of people?

I didn't realize that not long before this Sunday one of the young families of our church discovered that their child was being sexually abused by a close relative. It was incredibly traumatic. They were there that Sunday morning and sat under that message. I wonder how many advisers to us pastors today would have said: "Pastor Piper, can't you see your people are hurting? Can't you come down out of the heavens and get practical? Don't you realize what kind of people sit in front of you on Sunday?" Some weeks later I learned the story. The husband took me aside one Sunday after a service. "John," he said, "these have been the hardest months of our lives. Do you know what has gotten me through? The vision of the greatness of God's holiness that you gave me the first week of January. It has been the rock we could stand on."

The greatness and the glory of God are relevant. It

does not matter if surveys turn up a list of perceived needs that does not include the supreme greatness of the sovereign God of grace. That is the deepest need. Our people are starving for God.

Another illustration of this is the way missions mobilization is happening at our church, and the way it has happened again and again in history. Young people today don't get fired up about denominations and agencies. They get fired up about the greatness of a global God, and about the unstoppable purpose of a sovereign King. The first great missionary said, "We have been given grace and apostleship to bring about the obedience of faith *for the sake of his name* among all the nations" (Rom. 1:5, emphasis added). Missions is for the sake of the name of God. It flows from a love for God's glory and for the honor of his reputation. It is an answer to the prayer, "Hallowed be thy name!"

So I am persuaded that the vision of a great God is the linchpin in the life of the church, both in pastoral care and missionary outreach. Our people need to hear God-entranced preaching. They need someone, at least once a week, to lift up his voice and magnify the supremacy of God. They need to behold the whole panorama of his excellencies. Robert Murray M'Cheyne said, "It is not great talents God blesses so much as great likeness to Jesus. A holy minister is an awful weapon in the hand of God."[1] In other words, what people need most is our personal holiness. Yes, and human holiness is nothing other than a God-immersed life—the living out of a God-entranced worldview.

God himself is the necessary subject matter of our preaching, in his majesty and truth and holiness and righteousness and wisdom and faithfulness and sovereignty and grace. I don't mean we shouldn't preach about nitty-gritty, practical things like parenthood and divorce and AIDS and gluttony and television and sex. What I mean is that every one of those things should be swept up into the holy presence of God and laid bare to the roots of its Godwardness or godlessness.

It is not the job of the Christian preacher to give people moral or psychological pep talks about how to get along in the world; someone else can do that. But most of our people have no one in the world to tell them, week in and week out, about the supreme beauty and majesty of God. And so many of them are tragically starved for the God-centered vision of that great preacher Jonathan Edwards.

Church historian Mark Noll finds it a tragedy that in the two and one-half centuries since Edwards, "American evangelicals have not thought about life from the ground up as Christians because their entire culture has ceased to do so. Edwards's *piety* continued on in the revivalist tradition, his *theology* continued on in academic Calvinism, but there were no successors to his God-entranced world-view or his profoundly theological philosophy. The disappearance of Edwards's perspective in American Christian history has been a tragedy."[2]

Charles Colson echoes this conviction: "The western church—much of it drifting, enculturated, and

infected with cheap grace—desperately needs to hear
Edwards's challenge . . . It is my belief that the
prayers and work of those who love and obey Christ
in our world may yet prevail as they keep the message
of such a man as Jonathan Edwards."[3]

The recovery of Edwards's "God-entranced world-
view" in the messengers of God would be a cause for
great rejoicing in the land, a reason for profound
thanksgiving to the God who makes all things new.

The material in Part 1 was first delivered as the
Harold John Ockenga Lectures on Preaching at Gordon-
Conwell Theological Seminary in February 1988. The
substance of Part 2 was first given as the Billy Graham
Center Lectures on Preaching at Wheaton College in
October 1984. This privilege and effort was far greater
gain to me than to anyone else; I thank the administra-
tive leaders at these schools who trusted me and
stretched my own grasp of the high calling of the
Christian preacher.

I continually thank God that he has never left me
on a Sunday morning without a word to speak and a
zeal to speak it for his glory. Oh, I have my moods.
My family of four sons and a steady wife is not without its pain and tears. Criticism can stab to the quick,
and discouragement can go so deep as to leave this
preacher numb. But it is a gift of measureless,
sovereign grace that, beyond all desert and all inade-
quacy, God has opened his Word to me and given me
a heart to savor it and send it forth week after week. I
have never ceased to love preaching.

In the mercy of God there is a human reason for
this. Charles Spurgeon knew it, and most happy

preachers know it. Once Spurgeon was asked about the secret of his ministry. After a moment's pause he responded, "My people pray for me."[4] This is why I have been revived again and again for the work of the ministry. This is how *The Supremacy of God in Preaching* came to be written. My people pray for me. To them I dedicate this book with affection and gratitude.

My prayer is that the book may turn the hearts of God's heralds to the fulfillment of this great apostolic admonition:

If someone speaks,
let it be as the oracles of God . . .
by the strength which God supplies;
that in everything God may be glorified
through Jesus Christ.
To him belong glory and dominion for ever and ever.
Amen.

[1 Pet. 4:11, author's translation]

JOHN PIPER

PART ONE

Why God Should Be Supreme in Preaching

1

The Goal of Preaching
The Glory of God

In September 1966 I was a junior pre-med student majoring in literature at Wheaton College. I had finished a chemistry course in summer school, was head-over-heels in love with Noël and was more sick than I have ever been before or since with mononucleosis. The doctor confined me to the health center for three of the most decisive weeks of my life. It was a time for which I do not cease to thank God.

Back in those days the fall semester began with Spiritual Emphasis Week. The speaker in 1966 was Harold John Ockenga. It was the first and last time I ever heard him preach. WETN, the college radio station, carried the sermons, and I listened as I lay on my bed two hundred yards from his pulpit. Under the preaching of the Word by Pastor Ockenga the direction of my life was permanently changed. I can remember my heart almost bursting with longing as I listened—longing to know and handle the Word of God like that. Through those messages God called me to the ministry of the Word, irresistibly and (I believe) irrevocably. It has been my conviction ever since that the subjective evidence of God's call to the ministry of the Word (to quote Charles Spurgeon) "is an intense, all-absorbing desire for the work."[1]

When I got out of the health center, I dropped organic chemistry, took up philosophy as a minor, and set my face to get the best biblical and theological education I could. Twenty-two years later (at this lecture in 1988) I can testify that the Lord has never let me doubt that call. It rings as clear in my heart today as it ever has. And I simply stand in awe at the gracious providence of God—to save me and call me as a servant of the Word, and then two decades later to let me speak under the banner of The Harold John Ockenga Lectures on Preaching at Gordon-Conwell Theological Seminary.

This, then, is a precious privilege for me. I pray that it will be an acceptable tribute to Dr. Ockenga, who never knew me—and therefore a testimony to the fact that the true usefulness of our preaching will not be known to us until each fruit on all the branches on all the trees that have sprung up from all the seeds we've sown has fully ripened in the sunshine of eternity.

> For as the rain and the snow come down from heaven,
> and return not thither but water the earth,
> making it bring forth and sprout,

giving seed to the sower and bread to the eater,
so shall my word be that goes forth from my mouth;
it shall not return to me empty,
but it shall accomplish that which I purpose,
and prosper in the thing for which I sent it.
(Isa. 55:10–11)

Dr. Ockenga never knew what his preaching did in my life, and you can mark it down that if you are a preacher God will hide from you much of the fruit he causes in your ministry. You will see enough to be assured of his blessing, but not so much as to think you could live without it. For God aims to exalt himself, not the preacher. That brings us to the main theme: The Supremacy of God in Preaching. Its outline is intentionally trinitarian:

The Goal of Preaching: *the Glory of God*
The Ground of Preaching: *the Cross of Christ*
The Gift of Preaching: *the Power of the Holy Spirit*

God the Father, God the Son, and God the Holy Spirit are the beginning, middle, and end in the ministry of preaching. Written over all ministerial labor, especially preaching, stand the words of the apostle: "From him and through him and to him are all things. To him be glory for ever" (Rom. 11:36).

The Scottish preacher James Stewart said the aims of all genuine preaching are "to quicken the conscience by the holiness of God, to feed the mind with the truth of God, to purge the imagination by the beauty of God, to open the heart to the love of God, to devote the will to the purpose of God."[2] In other

19

words, God is the goal of preaching, God is the ground of preaching—and all the means in between are given by the Spirit of God.

My burden is to plead for the supremacy of God in preaching—that the dominant note of preaching be the freedom of God's sovereign grace, the unifying theme be the zeal that God has for his own glory, the grand object of preaching be the infinite and inexhaustible being of God, and the pervasive atmosphere of preaching be the holiness of God. Then when preaching takes up the ordinary things of life—family, job, leisure, friendships; or the crises of our day—AIDS, divorce, addictions, depression, abuses, poverty, hunger, and, worst of all, unreached peoples of the world, these matters are not only taken up. They are taken all the way up into God.

John Henry Jowett, who preached for thirty-four years in England and America until 1923, saw this as the great power of such nineteenth-century preachers as Robert Dale, John Newman, and Charles Spurgeon: "They were always willing to stop at the village window, but they always linked the streets with the heights, and sent your souls a-roaming over the eternal hills of God . . . It is this note of vastitude, this ever-present sense and suggestion of the Infinite, which I think we need to recover in our preaching."[3] Nearing the end of the twentieth century the need for that recovery is ten times as great.

Nor am I here proposing a kind of artsy elitist preoccupation with philosophical or intellectual imponderables. There are esthetic types who gravitate to high church services because they can't stand the "slapstick" of evangelical worship. Spurgeon was anything but an intellectual elitist. There has scarcely been a pastor with more popular appeal. His messages, however, were full of God and the atmosphere was charged with the presence of awesome realities. "We shall never have great preachers," he said, "till we have great divines."[4]

That wasn't because he cared more about great ideas than lost souls; he cared about the one because he loved the other. It was the same with Isaac Watts, who lived a hundred years earlier. Samuel Johnson said of Watts, "Whatever he took in hand was, by his incessant solicitude for souls, converted to theology."[5] I take this to mean in Watts's case that everything was brought into relation to God because he cared about people.

Today Johnson would, I believe, say of much contemporary preaching, "Whatever the preacher takes in his hand is, by his incessant solicitude for relevance, converted to psychology." Neither the great aims of preaching nor the worthy place of psychology is honored in this loss of theological nerve. One reason why people sometimes doubt the abiding value of God-centered preaching is because they have never heard any. J. I. Packer tells about how he heard the preaching of D. Martyn Lloyd-Jones every Sunday evening at Westminster Chapel during 1948 and 1949. He said that he had never heard such preaching. It came to him with the force and surprise of electric shock. Lloyd-Jones, he said, brought him "more of a sense of God than any other man."[6]

Is this what people take away from worship nowadays—a sense of God, a note of sovereign grace, a theme of panoramic glory, the grand object of God's infinite Being? Do they enter for one hour in the week—not an excessive expectation—into an atmosphere of the holiness of God which leaves its aroma upon their lives all week long?

Cotton Mather, who ministered in New England 300 years ago, said, "The great design and intention of the office of a Christian preacher [is] to restore the throne and dominion of God in the souls of men."[7] That was not a rhetorical flourish. It was a measured and accurate exegetical conclusion from one of the great biblical texts which leads to the biblical foundation for God's supremacy in preaching. The text behind Mather's statement is Romans 10:14–15: "How are men to call upon him in whom they have not believed? And how are they to believe in him of whom they have never heard? And how are they to hear without a preacher? And how will they preach unless they are sent? As it is written, 'How beautiful are the feet of those who preach good news!'" From this text preaching could be defined as *the heralding of good news from a messenger sent by God.* ("Heralding"—from the word *kērussontos* in verse 14; "of good news"—from *euangelizomenōn agatha* in verse 15; "sent by a sent messenger"—from *apostalōsin* in verse 15.)

The key question is: What does the preacher herald? What is the good news referred to here? Since verse 16 is a quotation of Isaiah 52:7, we do well to go back and let Isaiah define it for us. Listen for what

Mather heard in this verse concerning the great design of Christian preaching:

> How beautiful upon the mountains are the feet of him
> who brings good tidings,
> who publishes peace,
> who brings good tidings of good,
> who publishes salvation,
> who says to Zion, "Your God reigns."

The good tidings of the preacher, the peace and salvation that he publishes, are boiled down into one sentence: "Your God Reigns!" Mather applies this, with full justification, to the preacher: "The great design . . . of a Christian preacher [is] to restore the throne and dominion of God in the souls of men."

The keynote in the mouth of every prophet-preacher, whether in Isaiah's day or Jesus' day or our day, is "Your God Reigns!" God is the King of the universe; he has absolute creator rights over this world and everyone in it. Rebellion and mutiny are on all sides, however, and his authority is scorned by millions. So the Lord sends preachers into the world to cry out that God reigns, that he will not suffer his glory to be scorned indefinitely, that he will vindicate his name in great and terrible wrath. But they are also sent to cry that for now a full and free amnesty is offered to all the rebel subjects who will turn from their rebellion, call on him for mercy, bow before his throne, and swear allegiance and fealty to him forever. The amnesty is signed in the blood of his Son.

So Mather is absolutely right: The grand design of

the Christian preacher is to restore the throne and dominion of God in the souls of men. But why? Can we go deeper? What is driving the heart of God in demanding that we submit to his authority and in offering the mercy of amnesty?

Isaiah gives the answer in an earlier text. Speaking of his mercy to Israel, God says,

> For my name's sake I defer my anger,
> for the sake of my praise I restrain it for you,
> that I may not cut you off.
> Behold, I have refined you, but not like silver,
> I have tried you in the furnace of affliction.
> For my own sake, for my own sake, I do it,
> for how should my name be profaned?
> My glory I will not give to another.
>
> [Isa. 48:9–11]

Behind and beneath the sovereign exercises of God's mercy as king is an unwavering passion for the honor of his name and the display of his glory.

So we can go deeper than Mather's point. Behind God's commitment to reign as King is the deeper foundational commitment that his glory will one day fill the earth (Num. 14:21; Isa. 11:9; Hab. 2:14; Pss. 57:5; 72:19). This discovery has a tremendous implication for preaching, for God's deepest purpose for the world is to fill it with reverberations of his glory in the lives of a new humanity, ransomed from every people, tribe, tongue, and nation (Rev. 5:9).[8] But the glory of God does not reflect brightly in the hearts of men and women when they cower unwillingly in submission to his authority or when they obey in servile fear or when there is no gladness in response to the glory of their King.

The implication for preaching is plain: When God sends his emissaries to declare, "Your God reigns!" his aim is not to constrain man's submission by an act of raw authority; his aim is to ravish our affections with irresistible displays of glory. The only submission that fully reflects the worth and glory of the King is glad submission. Begrudging submission berates the King. No gladness in the subject, no glory to the King.

This is what Jesus said in effect in Matthew 13:44, "The kingdom [the rule, the dominion] of heaven is like treasure hidden in a field, which a man found and covered up; then in his joy [his glad submission to that kingship and his delight in its glory, its value] he goes and sells all that he has and buys that field." When the kingdom is a treasure, submission is a pleasure. Or to turn it around, when submission is a pleasure, the kingdom is glorified as a treasure. Therefore, if the goal of preaching is to glorify God, it must aim at glad submission to his kingdom, not raw submission.

Paul said in 2 Corinthians 4:5, "For what we preach is not ourselves but Jesus Christ as Lord." But then in verse 6 he goes beneath that proclamation of the lordship of Christ—beneath the rule and authority of King Jesus—and tells the essence of his preaching: it is "the light of the knowledge of the glory of God in the face of Christ." The only submission to the lordship of Christ that fully magnifies his worth and reflects his beauty is the humble gladness of the human soul in the glory of God in the face of his Son.

The wonder of the gospel and the most freeing discovery this sinner has ever made is that God's deepest commitment to be glorified and my deepest longing to be satisfied are not in conflict, but in fact find simultaneous consummation in his display of and my delight in the glory of God.[9] Therefore the goal of preaching is the glory of God reflected in the glad submission of the human heart. And the supremacy of God in preaching is secured by this fact: The one who satisfies gets the glory; the one who gives the pleasure is the treasure.

2

The Ground of Preaching
The Cross of Christ

Preaching is the heralding of the good news by a
messenger sent by God, the good news . . .

that God reigns;

that he reigns to reveal his glory;

that his glory is revealed most fully in the glad submission of his creation;

that there is, therefore, no final conflict between
God's zeal to be glorified and our longing to be
satisfied,

and that someday the earth will be filled with the
glory of the Lord, echoing and reverberating in
the white-hot worship of the ransomed church
gathered in from every people and tongue and
tribe and nation.

The goal of preaching is the glory of God reflected in
the glad submission of his creation.

But there are two massive obstacles to the attainment of this goal: the righteousness of God and the pride of man. The righteousness of God is his unwavering zeal for the exaltation of his glory.[1] The pride of man is his unwavering zeal for the exaltation of *his* glory.

What in God is righteousness, in man is sin. This is the very point of Genesis 3—sin came into the world through a temptation, and the essence of that temptation was: "You will be like God." The effort to imitate God at this point is the essence of our corruption.

Our parents fell for it, and in them we have all fallen for it. It is now part of our nature. We take the mirror of God's image which was intended to reflect his glory in the world, turn our backs to the light, and fall in love with the contours of our own dark shadow, trying desperately to convince ourselves (with technological advances or management skills or athletic prowess or academic achievements or sexual exploits or countercultural hair styles) that the dark shadow of the image on the ground in front of us is really glorious and satisfying. In our proud love affair with ourselves we pour contempt, whether we know it or not, on the worth of God's glory.

As our pride pours contempt upon God's glory, his righteousness obliges him to pour wrath upon our pride.

The haughty looks of man shall be brought low,
and the pride of men shall be humbled;
and the Lord alone will be exalted in that day.
For how should my name be profaned?

My glory I will not give to another.
The eyes of the haughty are humbled . . .
and the Holy God shows himself holy in righteous-
    ness.
Destruction is decreed,
overflowing with righteousness . . .
                    [Isa. 2:11; 48:11; 5:15–16; 10:22]

The goal of preaching is the glory of God in the glad submission of his creation. And so there is an obstacle to this preaching in God and there is an obstacle in man. The pride of man will not delight in God's glory, while the righteousness of God will not suffer his glory to be scorned.

So where is there any hope that preaching might attain its goal—that God be glorified in those who are satisfied in him? Can the righteousness of God ever relent in its opposition to sinners? Can the pride of man ever be broken of its own vanity and be satisfied in God's glory? Is there a basis for such hope? Is there a ground for valid and hopeful preaching?

There is. In the cross of Christ God has undertaken to overcome both obstacles to preaching. It overcomes the objective, external obstacle of God's righteous opposition to human pride, and it overcomes the subjective, internal obstacle of our proud opposition to God's glory. In so doing the cross becomes the ground of the objective validity of preaching and the ground of the subjective humility of preaching.

Let's take these one at a time and look at the biblical evidence.

The Cross as the Ground of the Validity of Preaching

The most fundamental problem of preaching is how a preacher can proclaim hope to sinners in view of God's unimpeachable righteousness. Of course, man by himself does not view this as the most serious problem. He never has.

R. C. Sproul made this point powerfully in a sermon on Luke 13:1–5 called "The Misplaced Locus of Amazement." Some people came to Jesus and told him about the Galileans whose blood Pilate had mingled with their sacrifices. Jesus responded in shockingly unsentimental words: "Do you think that these Galileans were worse sinners than all the other Galileans, because they suffered thus? I tell you, No; but unless you repent you will all likewise perish." In other words, Jesus says, "Are you amazed that a few Galileans were killed by Pilate? What you ought to be amazed at is that all of you haven't been killed, and that you will be someday if you don't repent."

Sproul pointed out that here is the age-old difference between the way natural man sees the problem of his relation to God and the way the Bible sees the problem of man's relation to God. Man-centered humans are amazed that God should withhold life and joy from his creatures. But the God-centered Bible is amazed that God should withhold judgment from sinners. One of the implications this has for preaching is that preachers who take their cue from the Bible and not from the world will always be wrestling with spiritual realities that many of their hearers do not even know exist or think essential. But the main point is that the fundamental problem with preaching, whether a man-centered age like ours feels it or not, is how a preacher can proclaim hope to sinners in view of God's unimpeachable righteousness.

And the glorious solution to that problem is the atonement that happened on the cross, as is set forth in this paraphrase of Romans 3:23–26:

> 23All have sinned and fall short of the glory of God [they exchanged the glory of God for the glory of the creature—Rom. 1:23]. 24They are justified freely by his grace through the redemption which is in Christ Jesus, 25whom God put forward as a propitiation through faith, by his blood [There's the cross!], for the demonstration of his righteousness on account of the passing over of sins done beforehand, 26in the forbearance of God; for a demonstration of his righteousness in the present time, in order that he might be both just and the one who justifies the one who has faith in Jesus.

What this amazing passage says is that the fundamental problem of preaching has been overcome by the cross. Without the cross the righteousness of God would demonstrate itself only in the condemnation of sinners, and the goal of preaching would be aborted—God would not be glorified in the gladness of his sinful creatures. His righteousness would simply be vindicated in their destruction.

What the text teaches is that—even though all scorn the glory of God (according to Rom. 3:23), and even though God's righteousness is his unwavering commitment to uphold that glory (implied in 3:25)—nevertheless God designed a way to vindicate the worth of his glory and at the same time to give hope to sinners who have scorned that glory. What he designed was the death of his Son. It took the infinitely costly death of the Son of God to repair the dishonor that my pride has brought upon the glory of God.

It horribly skews the meaning of the cross when contemporary prophets of self-esteem say that the cross is a witness to my infinite worth, since God was willing to pay such a high price to get me. The biblical perspective is that the cross is a witness to the infinite worth of God's glory, and a witness to the immensity of the sin of my pride. What should shock us is that we have brought such contempt upon the worth of God that the very death of his Son is required to vindicate that worth. The cross stands in witness to the infinite worth of God and the infinite outrage of sin.

Therefore, what God achieved in the cross of Christ is the warrant or ground of preaching. Preaching would not be valid without the cross. The goal of preaching would contain an irresolvable contradiction—the glory of a righteous God magnified in the gladness of a sinful people. But the cross has brought together two sides of the goal of preaching which looked hopelessly at odds with each other: the vindication and exaltation of God's glory and the hope and gladness of sinful man.

In chapter 1 we saw that preaching is the heralding of the good news that God's zeal to be glorified and our longing to be satisfied are not in final conflict. And what we have seen so far in this chapter is that the ground of this proclamation is the cross of Christ.

This is the gospel beneath all the other things preaching has to say. Without the cross, preaching that aims to glorify a righteous God in the gladness of sinful man has no validity.

The Cross as the Ground of the Humility of Preaching.

The cross is also the ground of the humility of preaching because the cross is the power of God to crucify the pride of both preacher and congregation. In the New Testament the cross is not only a past place of objective substitution; it is also a present place of subjective execution—the execution of my self-reliance and my love affair with the praise of man. "Far be it from me to glory except in human cross Lord Jesus Christ, by which the world has been crucified to me, and I to the world" (Gal. 6:14).

The point where Paul makes the most of this crucifying power of the cross is in relation to his own preaching. I doubt that there is a more important passage on preaching in all the Bible than the first and second chapters of 1 Corinthians, where Paul shows that the great obstacle to the aims of preaching in Corinth was pride. The people are enamored with oratorical skill and intellectual prowess and philosophical airs. They line up behind their favorite teachers and boast in men: "I belong to Paul!" "I belong to Apollos!" "I belong to Cephas!"

Paul's aim in these chapters is stated negatively in 1:29, "that no human being might boast in the presence of God," and positively in 1:31, "Let him who boasts, boast in the Lord" (NASB). In other words, Paul will not deny us the great satisfaction that comes from exulting in glory and reveling in greatness. We were made for that very pleasure. But neither will he deny to God the glory and the greatness that echo back to him when people boast in the Lord and not in man. Glut your desire to boast by boasting in the Lord.

Paul's aims are the aims of Christian preaching—the glory of God in the glad-hearted, Godward boast of Christians. But pride stands in the way. To remove it Paul talks about the effect of the cross on his own preaching. His main point is that the "word of the cross" (1:18) is the power of God to break the pride of man—both preacher and listener—and bring us to a glad reliance on the mercy of God and not on ourselves.

Let me give you just a few examples of this from the text: "For Christ did not send me to baptize but to preach the gospel, and not with eloquent wisdom, lest the cross of Christ be emptied" (1 Cor. 1:17). Why would the cross have been emptied if Paul had come with oratorical flourishes and displays of philosophical wisdom? It would have been emptied because he would have been cultivating the very boasting in man that the cross was meant to crucify. This is what I mean when I say that the cross is the ground of the humility of preaching.

Consider the same point in 2:1: "When I came to you, brethren, I did not come proclaiming to you the testimony of God in lofty words or wisdom." In other words he avoided the ostentation of oratory and intellect. Why? What was the ground of this demeanor in preaching? Verse 2 tells us plainly: "For I decided to know nothing among you except Jesus Christ and him crucified."

I think what he means is that he set his mind to be so saturated with the crucifying power of the cross that in everything he said and did, in all his preaching, there would be the aroma of death—death to self-reliance, death to pride, death to boasting in man. In this aroma of death the life that people would see would be the life of Christ, and the power that people would see would be the power of God.

Why? Why did he want people to see this and not himself? Verse 5 answers that it is so "your faith might not rest in the wisdom of men but in the power of God." In other words, that God (not the preacher!) might be honored in the trust of his people. That's the goal of preaching!

I conclude that the cross of Christ not only provides a foundation for the validity of preaching, enabling us to herald the good news that a righteous God can and will be glorified in the glad submission of sinners; the cross of Christ also provides a foundation for the humility of preaching. It is both a past event of substitution and a present experience of execution.

It holds up the glory of God in preaching, and it holds down the pride of man in the preacher. It is the foundation of our doctrine and the foundation of our demeanor.

Paul goes so far as to say that unless the preacher is

crucified the preaching is nullified (1 Cor. 1:17). What we are in preaching is utterly crucial to what we say. This is why I turn in chapter 3 to the enabling power of the Holy Spirit and in chapter 4 to the gravity and gladness of preaching.

3

The Gift of Preaching
The Power of the Holy Spirit

The supremacy of God in preaching demands that displaying and magnifying God's glory be our constant goal in preaching (chapter 1), and the all-sufficiency of the cross of God's Son be the conscious validation of our preaching and humiliation of our pride (chapter 2). None of this will occur, however, in us alone. The sovereign work of the Spirit of God must be the power in which all is achieved.

How utterly dependent we are on the Holy Spirit in the work of preaching! All genuine preaching is rooted in a feeling of desperation. You wake up on Sunday morning and you can smell the smoke of hell on one side and feel the crisp breezes of heaven on the other. You go to your study and look down at your pitiful manuscript, and you kneel down and cry, "God, this is so weak! Who do I think I am? What audacity to think that in three hours my words will be the odor of death to death and the fragrance of life to life (2 Cor. 2:16). My God, who is sufficient for these things?"

Phillips Brooks used to counsel young preachers with these words: "Never allow yourself to feel equal to your work. If you ever find that spirit growing on you, be afraid."[1] And one reason to be afraid is because your Father will break you and humble you. Is there any reason to think that God should fit you for the ministry of preaching any differently than he did Paul?

> We were so utterly, unbearably crushed that we despaired of life itself. 9Why, we felt that we had received the sentence of death; but that was to make us rely not on ourselves but on God who raises the dead. [2 Cor. 1:8–9]

> To keep me from being too elated by the abundance of revelations, a thorn was given me in the flesh . . . to keep me from being too elated. [2 Cor. 12:7]

The dangers of self-reliance and self-exaltation in the ministry of preaching are so insidious that God will strike us if he must in order to break us of our self-assurance and the casual use of our professional techniques.

So Paul preached "in weakness and in much fear and trembling"—reverent before the glory of the Lord, broken in his native pride, crucified with Christ, shunning the airs of eloquence and intellect. And what happened? There was a demonstration of the Spirit and power! (2:4)

Without this demonstration of Spirit and power in our preaching nothing of any abiding value will be achieved no matter how many people may admire our cogency or enjoy our illustrations or learn from our doctrine. The goal of preaching is the glory of God in the glad submission of his people. How is God to get the glory from an act that is so manifestly human? First Peter 4:10–11 gives a resounding answer to that question: "As each has received a gift, employ it for one another, as good stewards of God's varied grace: whoever speaks, as one who utters oracles of God; whoever renders service, as one who renders it by the strength which God supplies; in order that in everything God may be glorified through Jesus Christ. To him belong glory and dominion for ever and ever. Amen."

Peter says that when it comes to speaking and serving, speak the oracles of God in reliance on the *power* of God, and the result will be the *glory* of God. In preaching, the one who sets the agenda and gives the power gets the glory. So if the goal of preaching is to be attained, we simply must preach the Word inspired by the Spirit of God in the power given by the Spirit of God.

So let's focus on these two aspects of preaching— the oracles of God that the Spirit has inspired, and the power of God brought to us in the anointing of his Spirit. Unless we learn how to rely on the Word of the Spirit and the power of the Spirit in all lowliness and meekness, it is not God who will get the glory in our preaching.

Relying on the Gift of the Spirit's Word—the Bible

Oh, how much needs to be said about the use of the Bible in preaching! Relying on the Holy Spirit at this point means believing heartily that "all Scripture is inspired by God and profitable for teaching, for reproof, for correction, and for training in righteousness" (2 Tim. 3:16), believing that "no prophecy [which in the context of 2 Pet. 1:19 means *Scripture*] ever came by the impulse of man, but that men moved by the Holy Spirit spoke from God" (2 Pet. 1:21), and having strong confidence that the words of Scripture are "not taught by human wisdom but taught by the Spirit" (1 Cor. 2:13). Where the Bible is esteemed as the inspired and inerrant Word of God, preaching can flourish. But where the Bible is treated merely as a record of valuable religious insight, preaching dies.

But it is not automatic that preaching will flourish where the Bible is believed to be inerrant. Among evangelicals today there are other effective ways for the power and authority of biblical preaching to be undercut. There are subjectivist epistemologies that belittle propositional revelation. There are linguistic theories that cultivate an exegetical atmosphere of ambiguity. There is a kind of popular, cultural relativism that enables people to dispense flippantly with uncomfortable biblical teaching.

Where these kinds of things take root, the Bible will be silenced in the church, and preaching will become a reflection of current issues and religious opinions. Surely this is not what Paul meant when he said to Timothy, "I charge you in the presence of God and of Christ Jesus who is to judge the living and the dead, and by his appearing and his kingdom: preach the word" (2 Tim. 4:1–2).

The Word! There's the focus. All Christian preaching should be the exposition and application of biblical texts. Our authority as preachers sent by God rises and falls with our manifest allegiance to the text of Scripture. I say "manifest" because there are so many preachers who say they are doing exposition when they do not ground their assertions explicitly— "manifestly"—in the text. They don't show their people clearly that the assertions of their preaching are coming from specific, readable words of Scripture that the people can see for themselves.

One of the biggest problems I have with younger preachers I am called on to critique is that they fail to quote the texts that support the points they are making. It makes me wonder if they have been taught that you should get the drift of a text and then talk in your own words for thirty minutes. The effect of that kind of preaching is to leave people groping for the Word of God and wondering whether what you said is really in the Bible.

Instead, in the literate Western culture we need to get people to open their Bibles and put their fingers on the text.[2] Then we need to quote a piece of our text and explain what it means. Tell them which half of the verse it is in. People lose the whole drift of a message when they are groping to find where the pastor's ideas are coming from. Then we should quote another piece of the text and explain what it means. Our explanation will draw in other passages of Scripture.

Quote them! Don't say general things like, "As Jesus says in the Sermon on the Mount." Along the way or at the end we should urge it into their consciences with penetrating application.

We are simply pulling rank on people when we tell them, and don't show them from the text. This does not honor the Word of God or the work of the Holy Spirit. I urge you to rely on the Holy Spirit by saturating your preaching with the Word he inspired.

We should also rely on the Holy Spirit for help in interpreting the Word. Paul said in 1 Corinthians 2:13–14 that he interprets spiritual things to spiritual people (that is, those who possess the Spirit) because the natural man does not receive the things of the Spirit, "for they are folly to him." It takes the Holy Spirit to make us docile to the Bible. The work of the Holy Spirit in the process of interpretation is not to add information, but to give to us the discipline to study and the humility to accept the truth we find without twisting it. Often a desperately needed discovery or insight is the added grace of his providential guidance.

I urge you to be like John Wesley in this matter of relying on the Spirit in his Word, the Bible. He said: "O give me that book! At any price give me the book of God! I have it: here is knowledge enough for me. Let me be a man of one book."[3]

It is not that reading other books or knowing the contemporary world is unimportant, but the greater danger is to neglect the study of the Bible. When the pastor is out of seminary and in the church ministry there are no courses, no assignments, no teachers. There is only the pastor, his Bible, and his books. And the vast majority of preachers fall far short of the resolution that Jonathan Edwards made when he was in his twenties: "To study the Scriptures so steadily, constantly, and frequently, as that I may find, and plainly perceive, myself to grow in the knowledge of the same."[4]

The really effective preachers have been ever growing in the Word of God. Their delight is in the law of the Lord and on his law they meditate day and night. Spurgeon said of John Bunyan, "Prick him anywhere; and you will find that his blood is Bibline, the very essence of the Bible flows from him. He cannot speak without quoting a text, for his soul is full of the Word of God."[5] Ours should be too. That is what it means to rely on the gift of the Spirit's Word.

Relying on the Gift of the Spirit's Power

But there is also the actual experience of the Spirit's power in the event of preaching. 1 Peter 4:11 says, that the one who serves should do so in the power that God supplies, so God, not the servant, might get the glory. The one who gives the power gets the glory. How do you preach like this? Practically, what does it mean to do something—like preaching—in another person's power?

Paul observed this relationship in 1 Corinthians 15:10, "I worked harder than any of them, though it was not I, but the grace of God which is with me." In Romans 15:18 he said, "I will not venture to speak of anything except what Christ has wrought through me to win obedience from the Gentiles, by word and deed." How do you preach so that the preaching is a demonstration of God's power and not your own?

I am trying to learn the answer to that question in my own life and preaching. I have a long way to go before I could ever be satisfied with my preaching. I do not see the measure of fruit that I long to see. Revival and awakening have not come to my own congregation in the force and depth that I desire. I struggle with discouragement at the sin in our church and the weakness of our witness in a perishing world. So for me to say, "Here is how you preach in the power of the Holy Spirit," is a very risky thing. Yet I can describe where I am in the quest for this precious, indispensable experience.

There are five steps that I follow in seeking to preach not in my own strength but in the strength that God supplies. I sum them up with an acronym so that I can remember them when my mind is befogged by fear or distraction. The acronym is *APTAT.*

Picture me in my chair behind the pulpit at Bethlehem Baptist Church. The time is, say, 10:15 on Sunday morning. The offertory ends and one of my associates steps to the pulpit to read the text for the morning message before I come to preach. As he begins to read, I bow my head before the Lord for one last transaction before the sacred moment of preaching. I almost always put my heart through *APTAT* before the Lord.

1. I *Admit* to the Lord my utter helplessness without him. I affirm that John 15:5 is absolutely

true of me at this moment: "Apart from me you can do nothing." I affirm to God that my heart would not beat, my eyes could not see, my memory would fail without him. Without God I would be plagued with distraction and self-consciousness. Without God I would doubt his reality. I would not love the people nor feel awe at the truth I am about to speak. Without him the Word would fall on deaf ears, for who else can raise the dead? Without you, O God, I can do nothing.

2. Therefore, I *Pray* for help. I beg for the insight, power, humility, love, memory, and freedom I need to preach this message for the glory of God's name, the gladness of his people, and the ingathering of his elect. I accept the invitation, "Call upon me in the day of trouble; I will deliver you, and you shall glorify me" (Ps. 50:15). The beginning of this prayer is not at the point of delivery. The sermon's preparation was done in almost constant prayer for help, and I get up three and a half hours before the first service to spend two hours getting my heart as ready as I can before I come to the church. And during that time I search for a promise in the Word that will be the basis of the next step in *APTAT*.

3. I *Trust.* I trust not merely in a general way in God's goodness, but in a specific promise in which I can bank my hope for that hour. I find this kind of specific trust in a particular Word of God utterly essential to fight off the assault of Satan in those moments. Recently I

strengthened myself with Psalm 40:17, "As for me, I am poor and needy; but the LORD takes thought for me. Thou art my help and my deliverer; do not tarry, O my God." I memorize the verse early in the morning, recite it to myself in the moment before preaching, believe it, resist the devil with it, and . . .

4. I *Act* in the confidence that God will fulfil his Word. I can testify that, although the fullness of blessing I long to see has been delayed, God has met me and his people again and again in the display of his glory and the creation of glad submission to his will. This leads to the final step.

5. I *Thank* God. At the end of the message I express gratitude that he has sustained me and that the truth of his Word and the purchase of his cross have been preached in some measure in the power of his Spirit to the glory of his name.

4

The Gravity
and Gladness
of Preaching

Two hundred and fifty years ago Jonathan Edwards's preaching sparked a great awakening among the churches. He was a great theologian (some would say second to none in church history), a great man of God, and a great preacher. We can't copy him uncritically, but, oh, what we can learn from this man, especially about the weighty business of preaching!

From the time he was a young man he was overwhelmingly earnest and intense in all that he did. One of his college resolutions was, *"Resolved, to live with all my might while I live."* His preaching was totally serious from beginning to end. You will look in vain for one joke in the 1200 sermons that remain.

In one ordination sermon in 1744 he said, "If a minister has light without heat, and entertains his [hearers] with learned discourses, without a savour of the power of godliness, or any appearance of fervency of spirit, and zeal for God and the good of souls, he may gratify itching ears, and fill the heads of his people with empty notions; but it will not be very likely to teach their hearts, or save their souls."[1]

Edwards had an overwhelming conviction of the reality of the glories of heaven and horrors of hell that made his preaching utterly earnest. He came under severe criticism for his participation in the revival fervor. Boston clergy, such as Charles Chauncy, accused him and others of stirring up far too much emotion with their dreadful seriousness about eternity. Edwards responded,

If any of you that are heads of families, saw one of your children in a house that was all on fire over its head, and in eminent danger of being soon consumed in the flames, that seemed to be very insensible of its danger, and neglected to escape, after you had often spake to it, and called to it, would you go on to speak to it only in a cold and indifferent manner? Would not you cry aloud, and call earnestly to it, and represent the danger it was in, and its own folly in delaying, in the most lively manner you were capable of? Would not nature itself teach this, and oblige you to it? If you should continue to speak to it only in a cold manner, as you are wont to do in ordinary conversation about indifferent matters, would not those about you begin to think you were bereft of reason yourself? . . .

If [then] we who have the care of souls, knew what hell was, had seen the state of the damned, or by any other means, become sensible how dreadful their case was . . . and saw our hearers in eminent danger, and that they were not sensible of their danger . . . it would be morally impossible for us to avoid abundantly and most earnestly setting before them the dreadfulness of that misery they were in danger of . . . and warning them to fly from it, and even to cry aloud to them.[2]

From the testimonies of his contemporaries we know that Edwards's sermons were tremendously powerful in their effect on the people in his Northampton congregation. It was not because he was anything like the dramatic orator that George Whitefield was. In the days of the awakening he still wrote his sermons out in full and read them with few gestures.

Then where was his power? Sereno Dwight, who assembled Edwards's memoirs, attributed his success in part to "the deep and pervading solemnity of his mind. He had, at all times, a solemn consciousness of the presence of God. This was visible in his looks and his demeanor. It obviously had a controlling influence over all his preparations for the pulpit; and was most manifest in all his public services. Its effect on the audience was immediate and not to be resisted."[3] Dwight asked a man who had heard Edwards personally whether he was an eloquent preacher and learned that,

He had no studied varieties of the voice, and no strong emphasis. He scarcely gestured, or even moved; and he made no attempt by the elegance of his style, or the beauty of his pictures, to gratify the taste, and fascinate the imagination. But, if you mean by eloquence, the power of presenting an important truth before an audience, with overwhelming weight of argument, and with such intenseness of feeling, that the whole soul of the speaker is thrown into every part of the conception and delivery; so that the solemn attention of the whole audience is riveted, from the beginning to the close, and impressions are left that cannot be effaced; Mr. Edwards was the most eloquent man I ever heard speak.[4]

Intensity of feeling, the weight of argument, a deep and pervading solemnity of mind, a savor of the power of godliness, fervency of spirit, zeal for God—these are the marks of the "gravity of preaching." If there is one thing we can learn from Edwards, it is to take our calling seriously, not to trifle with the Word of God and the act of preaching.

In Scotland a hundred years after Edwards, a hypocritical pastor named Thomas Chalmers was converted in his little parish of Kilmany. He became a powerful force for evangelicalism and for world missions from his pastorate in Glasgow and from his lectern at the University of St. Andrews and then Edinburgh. His fame and power in the pulpit were legendary in his lifetime.

Yet, according to James Stewart, Chalmers preached "with a disconcertingly provincial accent, with an almost total lack of dramatic gesture, tied rigidly to his manuscript, with his finger following the written lines as he read."[5] Andrew Blackwood refers to Chalmers's "bondage to the manuscript and use of long sentences."[6] What, then, was his secret? James Alexander who was teaching at Princeton at that time asked John Mason on his return from Scotland why Chalmers was so effective, and Mason replied, "It is his blood-earnestness."[7]

I want to give as strong a conviction as words can convey that the work of preaching is to be done in "blood-earnestness." We are in no danger of mechanical imitation of Edwards and Chalmers and their Puritan fathers. We have fallen so far from their conception of preaching that we couldn't imitate it if we tried. I say "fallen" because, whether a manuscript should be read or whether a sermon should be two hours long, and its sentences complex and stories few, the fact is that the glory of these preachers was their earnestness—an earnestness that might be called gravity. Most people today have so little experience of deep, earnest, reverent, powerful encounters with God in preaching that the only associations that come to mind when the notion is mentioned are that the preacher is morose or boring or dismal or sullen or gloomy or surly or unfriendly.

If you endeavor to bring a holy hush upon people in a worship service, you can be assured that someone will say that the atmosphere is unfriendly or cold. All that many people can imagine is that the absence of chatter would mean the presence of stiff, awkward unfriendliness. Since they have little or no experience with the deep gladness of momentous gravity, they strive for gladness the only way they know how—by being light-hearted, chipper, and talkative.

Pastors have absorbed this narrow view of gladness and friendliness and now cultivate it across the land with pulpit demeanor and verbal casualness that make the blood-earnestness of Chalmers and the pervading solemnity of Edwards's mind unthinkable. The result is a preaching atmosphere and a preaching style plagued by triviality, levity, carelessness, flippancy, and a general spirit that nothing of eternal and infinite proportions is being done or said on Sunday morning.

If I were to put my thesis into a measured sentence it would go like this: Gladness and gravity should be woven together in the life and preaching of a pastor in such a way as to sober the careless soul and sweeten the burdens of the saints. I say "sweeten" because it connotes some of the poignancy of the gladness I have in mind, and sets it off from the glib and petty attempts to stir up lightheartedness in a congregation. Love for people does not take precious realities lightly (hence the call for gravity), and love for people does not load people with the burden of obedience without providing the strength of joy to help them carry it (hence the call for the gladness).

Gladness in preaching is an act of love. It continually amazes people when I say that if a pastor is to truly love his people he must diligently pursue his happiness in the ministry of the Word. People have been taught consistently that to be a loving person you must abandon the pursuit of your own joy. It's all right to get it as an unexpected and unpursued result of love (as if that were psychologically possible), but it is not all right to pursue your happiness.

I assert the opposite: If you are indifferent to your joy in ministry you are indifferent to an essential element of love. And if you try to abandon your joy in the ministry of the Word you strive against God and your people. Consider Hebrews 13:17: "Obey your leaders and submit to them; for they are keeping watch over your souls, as men who will have to give account. Let them do this joyfully (*meta charas*) and not sadly (*stenazontes*), for that would be of no advantage to you (*alusiteles gar humin touto*)."

A pastor who reads this cannot come away indifferent to his joy if he loves his people. The text says that joyless ministry is no advantage to a people. But love aims at the advantage of our people. Therefore love cannot neglect the cultivation of its own joy in the ministry of the Word. Peter puts it in the form of a command: "Tend the flock of God that is your charge, not under constraint but willingly, not for shameful gain but eagerly" (1 Peter 5:2–3). "Willingly" and "eagerly" are just different words for gladly.

One reason an essential element of love is the enjoyment of our work is that you can't consistently give what you don't have. If you don't give gladness, you don't give the gospel; you give legalism. A pastor who guts out his work in gladless "obedience" transmits that life to his people and the name of it is hypocrisy and legalistic bondage, not the freedom of those whose yoke is easy and whose burden is light.

Another reason is that a pastor who is not manifestly glad in God does not glorify God. He cannot make God look glorious if knowing and serving this God gives no gladness to his soul. A bored and unenthusiastic tour guide in the Alps contradicts and dishonors the majesty of the mountains.

So Phillips Brooks was right in his estimation that

for a preacher to succeed he must thoroughly enjoy his work, for its "highest joy is in the great ambition that is set before it, the glorifying of the Lord and the saving of the souls of men. No other joy on earth compares with that. . . . As we read the lives of all the most effective preachers of the past, or as we meet the men who are powerful preachers of the Word today, we feel how certainly and how deeply the very exercise of their ministry delights them."[8]

The gladness of preaching is biblically essential if we would love men and glorify God—and these are the two great ends of preaching.

But what a difference there is between the joy of Edwards and the smiles and jokes of so many pastors in whom the strands of happiness are not woven together with a holy gravity. Edwards said: "All gracious affections, that are a sweet odor to Christ, and that fill the soul of a Christian with a heavenly sweetness and fragrancy, are brokenhearted affections. . . . The desires of the saints, however earnest, are humble desires: their hope is a humble hope; their joy, even when it is unspeakable, and full of glory, is a humble, brokenhearted joy. . . . "[9] There is something about the sheer weight of our sinfulness and the magnitude of God's holiness and the momentousness of our calling that should give a fragrance of humble gravity to the gladness of our preaching.

Gravity in preaching is appropriate because preaching is God's appointed means for the conversion of sinners, the awakening of the church, and the preservation of the saints. If preaching fails in its task, the consequences are infinitely terrible. "Since, in the wisdom of God, the world did not know God through wisdom, it pleased God through the folly of what we preach to save those who believe" (1 Cor. 1:21).

God saves people from everlasting ruin through preaching. When Paul ponders this in 2 Corinthians 2:15–16 he feels the overwhelming weight of this responsibility: "We are the aroma of Christ to God among those who are being saved and among those who are perishing, to one a fragrance from death to death, to the other a fragrance from life to life. Who is sufficient for these things?"

This is simply stupendous to think about—that when I preach the everlasting destiny of sinners hangs in the balance! If a person is not made earnest and grave by this fact, people will unconsciously learn that the realities of heaven and hell are not serious. I can't help but think that this is what is being communicated by the casual cleverness that comes from so many pulpits. James Denney said, "No man can give the impression that he himself is clever and that Christ is mighty to save."[10] John Henry Jowett said, "We never reach the innermost room in any man's soul by the expediencies of the showman or the buffoon."[11] And yet many preachers believe they must say something cute or clever or funny.

There actually seems to be a fear of approaching Chalmers's blood-earnestness. I have seen a strange silence begin to come over a congregation and watched the preacher, seemingly intentionally, dispel it quickly with some light-hearted quip or the use of a pun or a witticism.

Laughter seems to have replaced repentance as the

goal of many preachers. Laughter means people feel good. It means they like you. It means you have moved them. It means you have some measure of power. It seems to have all the marks of successful communication—if the depth of sin and the holiness of God and the danger of hell and need for broken hearts is left out of account. I have been literally amazed at conferences where preachers mention the need for revival and then proceed to cultivate an atmosphere in which it could never come. In recent months I have been reading *Lectures on Revivals* by William Sprague, and the memoirs of Asahel Nettleton, a powerful evangelist in the Second Great Awakening.

Deep and abiding spiritual awakening in these revivals was attended by a Spirit-given seriousness among the people of God. Some lines from Nettleton's Memoirs:

> Fall of 1812, South Salem, Connecticut: "His preaching produced an immediate solemnity on the minds of the people . . . The seriousness soon spread through the place, and the subject of religion became the engrossing topic of conversation." Spring of 1813, North Lyme: "There was no special seriousness when he commenced his labors. But a deep solemnity soon pervaded the congregation." August, 1814, East Granby: "The effect of his entrance into the place was electric. The schoolhouse . . . was filled with trembling worshippers. A solemnity and seriousness pervaded the community."[12]

The very first thing Sprague mentions in his chapter on the means of producing and promoting revivals is seriousness:

> I appeal to any of you who have been in the midst of a revival, whether a deep solemnity did not pervade the scene . . . And if you at such a moment have wished to be gay, have you not felt that was not the place for it? . . . It were worse than preposterous to think of carrying forward such a work by any means which are not marked by the deepest seriousness, or to introduce any thing which is adapted to awaken and cherish the lighter emotions, when all such emotions should be awed out of the mind. All ludicrous anecdotes, and modes of expression, and gestures, and attitudes, are never more out of place than when the Holy Spirit is moving upon the hearts of a congregation. Every thing of this kind is fitted to grieve him away; because it directly contradicts the errand on which he has come;—that of convincing sinners of their guilt, and renewing them to repentance.[13]

In spite of this historical reality that seems so obvious from the very nature of things even preachers who bemoan the absence of revival in our day seem locked into a cavalier demeanor in front of a group of people. Sometimes it seems that levity is the greatest enemy of any true spiritual work being done in the hearers.

Charles Spurgeon had a deep and robust sense of humor. He could use it for great effect. Robertson Nicoll, however, wrote about Spurgeon three years after the great preacher's death: "Evangelism of the humorous type may attract multitudes but it lays the soul in ashes and destroys the very germs of religion. Mr. Spurgeon is thought by those who do not know his sermons to have been a humorous preacher. As a matter of fact there was no preacher whose tone was more uniformly earnest, reverent and solemn."[14]

Spurgeon is an especially helpful example because he believed so deeply in the proper place of humor and laughter. He said to his students: "We must conquer—some of us especially—our tendency to levity. A great distinction exists between holy cheerfulness, which is a virtue, and that general levity, which is a vice. There is a levity which has not enough heart to laugh, but trifles with everything; it is flippant, hollow, unreal. A hearty laugh is no more levity than a hearty cry."[15]

It is a sign of the age that we preachers are far more adept at humor than tears. The apostle Paul spoke of sinners in Philippians 3:18 with tears because they lived their lives as "enemies of the cross of Christ." Without that weeping there will never be the revival we need, nor deep and lasting spiritual renewal.

Would there not come upon a congregation a powerful spirit of love and conviction if a pastor, with all earnestness and gravity, could begin his Easter sermon not with a joke or a cute story, but with the words of John Donne: "What Sea could furnish my eyes with tears enough to pour out, if I should think, that of all this congregation, which looks me in the face now, I should not meet one at the Resurrection, at that right hand of God!"[16]

Gravity and earnestness in preaching is appropriate, not only (as we have seen) because preaching is God's instrument for the weighty business of saving sinners and reviving his church, but also because it is God's instrument for preserving the saints. Paul says in 2 Timothy 2:10, "I endure everything for the sake of the elect, that they also may obtain the salvation which in Christ Jesus goes with eternal glory." Labor on behalf of the elect, therefore, is not icing on the cake of their eternal security. It is God's appointed means of keeping them secure. Eternal security is a community project (Heb. 3:12–13) and preaching is part of God's securing power. He calls effectually by the Word and he keeps effectually by the Word.

We can say that eternal security is certain for the Christian, yet avoid a mechanical view that drains the blood-earnestness right out of the weekly ministry of preaching to the saints. Biblically God uses the earnest application of the means of grace to hold his people secure; one of those means is the preaching of God's Word. Heaven and hell are at stake every Sunday morning not merely because unbelievers might be present, but also because our people are saved "IF they continue in the faith" (Col. 1:23). Paul connects the steadfastness of faith with the preaching of the Word of God in the gospel (Rom. 10:17).

Surely every preacher should say, with all gravity, "Who is sufficient for these things"—to save sinners, to revive the church, to preserve the saints! So I repeat my thesis: Gladness and gravity should be woven together in the life and preaching of a pastor in such a way as to sober the careless soul and sweeten the burdens of the saints. Love for people cannot treat awesome realities lightly (hence, gravity), and love for people cannot load people with the burden of joyless obedience (hence, gladness). Seven practical suggestions follow for cultivating this gravity and gladness in your preaching.

First, strive for practical, earnest, glad-hearted holiness in every area of your life. One of the reasons is that you can't be something in the pulpit that you aren't during the week—at least not for long. You can't be blood-earnest in the pulpit and habitually flippant at the deacons' meeting and the church dinner. Nor can you display the glory of God in the gladness of your preaching if you are surly and dismal and unfriendly during the week. Don't strive to be a kind of preacher. Strive to be a kind of person!

Second, make your life—especially the life of your study—a life of constant communion with God in prayer. The aroma of God will not linger on a person who does not linger in the presence of God. Richard Cecil said that "the leading defect in Christian ministers is the want of devotional habit."[17] We are called to the ministry of the word *and prayer*, because without prayer the God of our studies will be the unfrightening and uninspiring God of insipid academic gamesmanship.

Fruitful study and fervent prayer live and die together. B. B. Warfield once heard a person say that ten minutes on your knees will give you a truer, deeper knowledge of God than ten hours over your books. His response was exactly right: "What! than ten hours over your books on your knees?"[18] And the same should be true in the actual preparation of our sermons. Cotton Mather's rule was to stop at the end of every paragraph as he wrote his sermon to pray and examine himself and try to fix on his heart some holy impression of his subject.[19] Without this spirit of constant prayer, we cannot maintain the gravity and gladness that lingers in the vicinity of the throne of grace.

Third, read books written by those who bleed Bible when you prick them and who are blood-earnest about the truths they discuss. In fact I found it to be life-changing advice when a wise seminary professor told us to find one great evangelical theologian and immerse ourselves in his life and writing. I can scarcely overstate the effect it has had on my life to live with Jonathan Edwards month in and month out since my seminary days. And through him to find my way into the most earnest men in the world—Calvin, Luther, Bunyan, Burroughs, Bridges, Flavel, Owen, Charnock, Gurnall, Watson, Sibbes, and Ryle! Find the books that are blood-earnest about God, and you will discover they know the path that leads to joy more accurately than many contemporary guides.

Fourth, direct your mind often to the contemplation of death. It is absolutely inevitable if the Lord tarries, and it is utterly momentous. Not to think on its implications for life and preaching is incredibly naive. Edwards was the man he was—with depth and power (and eleven believing children!)—because of resolutions like these he made as a young man:

> 9. *Resolved,* To think much, on all occasions, of my dying, and of the common circumstances which attend death.
> 55. *Resolved,* To endeavor to my utmost, so to act, as I can think I should do, if I had already seen the happiness of heaven and torments of hell.[20]

Every funeral I perform is a deeply sobering experience. I sit there before my message and imagine myself or my wife or sons in that coffin. Death and sickness have an amazing way of blowing the haze of triviality out of life and replacing it with the wisdom of gravity and gladness in the hope of resurrection joy.

Fifth, consider the biblical teaching that as a preacher you will be judged with greater strictness. "Let not many of you become teachers, my brethren, for you know that we who teach shall be judged with greater strictness" (James 3:1). The writer of Hebrews says of pastors, "They are keeping watch over your souls, as men who will have to give account" (13:17). And Paul puts it most ominously in Acts 20 when he says to the people that he has been teaching in Ephesus, "I am innocent of the blood of all of you, for I did not shrink from declaring to you the whole counsel of God" (Acts 20:26–27). Evidently, not to teach God's counsel with fullness and faithfulness can leave the blood of our people on our hands. If we consider these things as we should, the gravity of the responsibility and the gladness of its successful outcome will shape everything we do.

Sixth, consider the example of Jesus. He was as kind and tender and gentle as a righteous man could be. He was not morose. They said John the Baptist had a demon; they said Jesus was a glutton and a drunkard, a friend of tax collectors and sinners. He was not a psychopathic killjoy, but he was a man of sorrows and acquainted with grief. He never preached a careless sermon, and there is no record of a careless word. He never told a joke that we know of, and all his humor was a sheath for the blood-earnest rapier of truth. Jesus is the great example for preachers—the crowds heard him gladly, the children sat in his lap, the women were honored. Yet no one in the Bible spoke of hell more often or in more horrible terms.

Seventh, strive with all your strength to know God and to humble yourself under his mighty hand (1 Pet. 5:6). Don't be content to guide people among the foothills of his glory. Become a mountain climber on the cliffs of God's majesty, and let the truth begin to overwhelm you so that you will never exhaust the heights of God. Every time you climb over a rim of insight there stretches out before you, disappearing into the clouds, a thousand miles of massive beauty in the character of God. Set yourself to climb, and ponder the thought that everlasting ages of discovery in the infinite Being of God will not suffice to weaken your gladness in the glory of God or dull the intensity of gravity in his presence.

How to Make God Supreme in Preaching

Guidance from the Ministry of Jonathan Edwards

When I was in seminary, a wise professor told me that, in addition to the Bible, I ought to choose one great theologian and apply myself throughout life to understanding and mastering his thought—to sink at least one shaft deep into reality rather than always dabbling on the surface of things. I might, in time, be able to "converse" with this theologian as a kind of peer, and know at least one system with which to bring other ideas into fruitful dialogue. It was good advice.

The theologian I have devoted myself to is Jonathan Edwards. I owe him more than I can ever explain. He has fed my soul with the beauty of God and holiness and heaven when every other door seemed closed to me. He has renewed my hope and my vision for ministry in some very low times. He has opened the window on the world of the Spirit time and again when all I could see were the curtains of secularism. He has shown me the possibility of mingling rigorous thought about God with warm affection for God. He embodies the truth that theology exists for doxology. He could spend whole mornings in ejaculatory prayer walking in the woods outside Northampton. He had a passion for truth and a passion for lost sinners. All of this flourished in the pastorate. Above all, Edwards had a passion for God, which is why he is so important if we are to focus on the supremacy of God in preaching.

Jonathan Edwards preached the way he did because of the man he was and the God he saw. The following chapters will deal in turn with Edwards's life, theology, and preaching.

5

Keep God Central
The Life of Edwards

Jonathan Edwards was born in 1703 in Windsor, Connecticut. His father was the local pastor and taught his only son Latin when he turned six. At twelve Jonathan was sent off to Yale. Five years later he graduated with highest honors and gave the valedictory address in Latin.

He studied for the ministry for two more years at Yale, then took a brief pastorate at a Presbyterian church in New York. Beginning in 1723, Edwards tutored at Yale for three years. Then came the call to the Congregational church of Northampton, Massachusetts. Edwards's grandfather, Solomon Stoddard, had been pastor there for over half a century. He handpicked Edwards as his apprentice and successor. The partnership began in February 1727. Stoddard died in 1729. Edwards remained the pastor until 1750—a twenty-three year relationship.

Back in 1723 Edwards had fallen in love with a thirteen-year-old girl named Sarah Pierrepont who proved to be just the kind of woman who could share his religious transport. On the front page of his Greek grammar he wrote the only kind of love song of which his heart was capable: "They say there is a young lady in [New Haven] who is loved of that Great Being who made and rules the world. . . . She will sometimes go about from place to place, singing sweetly, and seems to be always full of joy and pleasure; and no one knows for what. She loves to be alone walking in the fields and groves, and seems to have someone invisible always conversing with her."[1]

Four years later, five months after his installation at Northampton, they were married. They had eleven children (eight daughters and three sons), all of whom revered their father and brought no reproach upon the family, in spite of having a father who spent as many as thirteen hours a day studying.

For better or worse, Edwards did not practice regular pastoral visitation among his people (620 communicants in 1735). He went if sent for by the sick. He preached frequently at private meetings in particular neighborhoods. He catechized the children. And he encouraged anyone under religious conviction to come to him in his study for counsel. His own judgment about himself was that he was not a gifted conversationalist and that he could do the greatest good to the souls of men, and most promote the cause of Christ, by preaching and writing.[2] At least during the early years of his Northampton pastorate, Edwards preached two sermons a week, one on Sunday and one on a weekday evening. Sermons in those days were generally an hour in length, but could last considerably longer.

When he was still in college Edwards had written seventy resolutions. Already we have seen a few of them, including one which says, *"Resolved,* To live with all my might while I do live."[3] For him that came to mean a passionate devotion to the study of divinity. He maintained an extremely rigorous study schedule. He said that he thought "Christ commended rising early in the morning by his rising from the grave very early."[4] So he rose generally between four and five to enter his study. He would always study with pen in hand, thinking out every insight and recording it in his countless notebooks. Even on his travels he would pin pieces of paper to his coat to remind himself of insights he had along the way.

In the evening, when most pastors are either exhausted on the couch or at a finance committee meeting, Edwards returned to his study after spending an hour with his children after dinner. There were exceptions. On January 22, 1734, he wrote in his diary, "I judge that it is best, when I am in a good frame for divine contemplation . . . that, ordinarily, I will not be interrupted by going to dinner, but will forego my dinner, rather than be broke off."[5]

That may sound unhealthy, especially for one whose six-foot-one-inch frame was never robust. But Edwards watched his diet and exercise with great care. Everything was calculated to optimize his efficiency and power in study. He abstained from every quantity and kind of food that made him sick or sleepy. In the winter he got his exercise by chopping firewood; in the summer he would ride horseback and walk in the fields.

Regarding these walks in the fields he once wrote, "Sometimes on fair days I find myself more particularly disposed to regard the glories of the world than to betake myself to the study of serious religion."[6] So he had his struggles too. But for Edwards it wasn't a struggle between nature and God, but between two different experiences of God:

> Once as I rode out into the woods for my health in 1737, having alighted from my horse in a retired place, as my manner commonly has been, to walk for divine contemplation and prayer, I had a view, that for me was extraordinary, of the glory of the Son of God, as Mediator between God and man, and his wonderful, great, full, pure and sweet grace and love and meek, gentle condescension . . . which continued, as near as I can judge, about an hour; which kept me the greater part of the time in a flood of tears, and weeping aloud."[7]

He had an extraordinary love for the glory of God in nature. The good effects of this love on his capacity to delight in the greatness of God and on the imagery of his preaching were tremendous.

Edwards committed some pastoral blunders which lit the fuse that eventually exploded in his dismissal from his church. For example, in 1744 he implicated some innocent young people in an obscenity scandal.

But what ended his pastorate was Edwards's courageous public repudiation of the long-standing tradition in New England that profession of saving faith was not required in order to be a communicant at the Lord's Supper. His grandfather had long defended the practice of admitting people to the Lord's Supper who did not give profession or evidence of having been regenerated. Stoddard saw the Supper as a converting ordinance. Edwards came to reject this as unbiblical and wrote a book to plead his case. But on Friday, June 22, 1750, the decision of dismissal was read, and on July 1 Edwards delivered his farewell sermon. He was forty-six years old and had served the church for half of his life.

During all those years he had been the primary human spark plug for the divine voltage that caused the Great Awakening in New England. There were unusual seasons of revival, especially in the years 1734 to 1735 and 1740 to 1742. Almost all of Edwards's works published during his Northampton days were devoted to interpreting, defending, and promoting what he believed was a surprising work of God and not mere emotional hysteria. This should help us to keep in mind that Edwards's preaching generally had a wider audience than his own parish. He always had in mind Christ's kingdom on earth and he knew his voice was reverberating beyond the borders of Northampton. Some of his works were published in Britain before they were published in Boston.

After his dismissal from Northampton, he accepted a call to Stockbridge in western Massachusetts as pastor of the church and missionary to the Indians. He worked there until 1758, when he went to be president of Princeton.

These seven years in out-of-the-way Stockbridge were immensely productive for Edwards, and in 1757 he was just starting to feel at home. So on October 19, 1757, after being called to the presidency of Princeton, Edwards wrote to the trustees of Princeton to convince them that he was unfit for the job. He said, "I have a constitution, in many respects, peculiarly unhappy, attended with flaccid solids, vapid, sizy, and scarce fluids, and a low tide of spirits; often occasioning a kind of childish weakness and contemptibleness of speech, presence, and demeanor, with a disagreeable dulness and stiffness, much unfitting me for conversation, but more especially for the government of a college."

He added, "I am also deficient in some parts of learning, particularly in algebra, and the higher parts of mathematics, and the Greek classics; my Greek learning having been chiefly in the New Testament." One wonders how well he had preserved his Hebrew through thirty years of pastoral labor because he says that he would never want to spend his time teaching languages, "unless it be the Hebrew tongue; which I should be willing to improve myself in, by instructing others." But it was typical of the man that at fifty-four he desired to improve his grasp of the biblical languages. He spoke of the books he planned to write and then pleaded for release to do what his heart longed for: "My heart is so much in these studies, that I cannot find it in my heart to be willing to put myself into an incapacity to pursue them any more in the future part of my life."[8]

So when the council of ministers that Edwards had personally called to Stockbridge voted that it was his duty to accept the presidency, Edwards wept openly before the council but accepted their advice. He left almost immediately, and arrived at Princeton in January 1758. On February 13 he was inoculated for smallpox with apparent success. But secondary fever set in, large pustules formed on his throat which prevented his taking medications, and he died on March 22, 1758, at the age of fifty-four.

His last words to the grieving and fearful friends at his bedside were, "Trust in God and ye need not fear."[9] His great trust in the sovereign goodness of God perhaps found its most eloquent expression in the strength of his wife. She received word of her husband's death by letter from his physician. The first response recorded is the letter she wrote to her daughter Esther on April 3, two weeks after Edwards's death.

My very dear child!
What shall I say? A holy and good God has covered us with a dark cloud. O that we may kiss the rod, and lay our hands on our mouths! The Lord has done it. He has made me adore his goodness, that we had him so long. But my God lives; and he has my heart. O what a legacy my husband, and your father, has left us! We are all given to God; and there I am, and love to be.

Your ever affectionate mother,
SARAH EDWARDS[10]

6

Submit to Sweet Sovereignty
The Theology of Edwards

What Jonathan Edwards preached and *how* he preached were extensions of his vision of God. So before we discuss his preaching we need a glimpse of that vision. In 1735 Edwards preached a sermon on the text, "Be still and know that I am God" (Ps. 46:10). From the text he developed the following doctrine, "God doth not require us to submit contrary to reason, but to submit as seeing the reason and ground of submission.—Hence, the bare consideration *that God is God*, may well be sufficient to still all objections and opposition against the divine sovereign dispensations."[1]

When Jonathan Edwards became still and contemplated the great truth that *God is God*, he saw a majestic Being whose sheer existence implied infinite power, infinite knowledge, and infinite holiness. He went on to argue:

> It is most evident by the works of God, that his understanding and power are infinite. . . . Being thus infinite in understanding and power, he must also be perfectly holy; for unholiness always argues some defect, some blindness. Where there is no darkness or delusion, there can be no unholiness. . . . God being infinite in power and knowledge, he must be self-sufficient and all-sufficient; therefore it is impossible that he should be under any temptation to do any thing amiss; for he can have no end in doing it. . . . So God is essentially holy, and nothing is more impossible than that God should do amiss.[2]

For Edwards the infinite power, or absolute sovereignty, of God was the foundation of God's all-sufficiency. And this all-sufficiency is the fountain of his perfect holiness, and Edwards said in *A Treatise Concerning Religious Affections* that God's holiness comprehends all his moral excellency. So the sovereignty of God for Edwards was utterly crucial to everything else he believed about God.[3]

When he was twenty-six or twenty-seven, he looked back nine years to the time he fell in love with the doctrine of the sovereignty of God and wrote, "There has been a wonderful alteration in my mind, in respect to the doctrine of God's sovereignty, from that day to this . . . God's absolute sovereignty . . . is what my mind seems to rest assured of, as much as of any thing that I see with my eyes. . . . The doctrine has very often appeared exceeding pleasant, bright, and sweet.

Absolute sovereignty is what I love to ascribe to God
. . . God's sovereignty has ever appeared to me, [a] great
part of his glory. It has often been my delight to
approach God, and adore him as a sovereign God."[4]

As Edwards beheld God, and stood entranced by his
absolute sovereignty, he didn't see this reality in iso-
lation. It was part of God's glory. It was sweet to
Edwards because it was a great and vital part of an
infinitely glorious Person whom he loved with
tremendous passion.

Two inferences follow from this vision of God. The
first is that the goal of all that God does is to uphold
and display his glory. All God's actions flow from fullness, not from deficiency. Most human actions are
motivated by the need to make up some deficit or
supply some lack in ourselves. God never takes steps
to supply his insufficiency. He performs no remedial
exercises. As an absolutely sovereign and all-sufficient fountain, all his actions are the overflow of his
fullness. He never acts to add to his glory but only to
uphold it and display it. (This is unfolded masterfully
in *Dissertation Concerning the End for Which God
Created the World*.[5])

The other inference from his vision of God is that
the duty of man is to *delight* in God's glory. I focus on
the word *delight* intentionally because many people
in Edwards's day and in ours are willing to say that
the chief end of man is to glorify God and enjoy him
forever. But by and large they consider the enjoyment
of God optional and do not understand with Edwards
that the chief end of man is to glorify God *by* enjoy-
ing him forever.

Delight is what Edwards called an "affection" (we might say emotion). He wrote *A Treatise Concerning Religious Affections* to make one main point: "True religion, in great part, consists in holy affections." He defined affections as "the more vigorous and sensible exercises of the inclination and will of the soul"[6]—things like hatred, desire, joy, delight, grief, hope, fear, gratitude, compassion, and zeal.

When we speak of delight in God as our duty we must realize it is not a simple thing. One vigorous inclination in the human heart always must include others. Delight in the glory of God includes, for example, *hatred* for sin, *fear* of displeasing God, *hope* in the promises of God, *contentment* in the fellowship of God, *desire* for the final revelation of the Son of God, *exultation* in the redemption he accomplished, *grief* and contrition for failures of love, *gratitude* for undeserved benefits, *zeal* for the purposes of God, and *hunger* for righteousness. Our duty toward God is that all our affections respond properly to his reality and so reflect his glory.

Edwards was utterly convinced that there is no true religion without holy affections. "He who has no religious affection is in a state of spiritual death and is wholly destitute of powerful quickening influences of the Spirit of God."[7]

But not only that; there is no true religion (or true saint) where there is no *perseverance* in holy affections. Perseverance is the mark of the elect and necessary to final salvation. "They that will not live godly lives find out for themselves that they are not elected;

they that will live godly lives, have found out for themselves that they are elected."[8]

Edwards believed in justification by faith and thought much about how it related to perseverance. But the big issue then as now was: What is faith? Edwards said two crucial things. First, saving faith includes "belief of the truth, and an answerable disposition of the heart."[9] Since faith is an answerable disposition of the heart, it is not something different from the affections. Faith is "the soul's entirely embracing the revelation of Jesus Christ as our Savior." This embrace is an embrace of love: "faith arises . . . from a principle of divine love" (Cf. 1 Cor. 13:7; John 3:19; 5:42). "Love to God is the main thing in saving faith." In other words, faith arises "from a spiritual taste and relish of what is excellent and divine."[10] Therefore delight in God is the root of faith and faith is an essential expression of our delight in God. Contrary to much contemporary teaching, saving faith is by no means a mere decision of the will separate from the affections.

Second, saving faith is persevering faith. "For God has respect to perseverance as being virtually in the first act [of saving faith]. And it is looked upon as if it were a property of that faith by which the sinner is then justified."[11] In other words, the first act of saving faith is like an acorn that has within it the spreading oak of all the subsequent perseverance which the Bible says is necessary for final salvation. We are justified by faith once for all at our conversion, but we must (and most certainly will) also persevere in the holy affections given to us in seed form at our conversion.

Therefore, Edwards said that "there is as much need of persons exercising care and diligence to persevere in order to their salvation, as there is of their attention and care to repent and be converted."[12] This had tremendous implications for the way Edwards preached. He saw preaching as a means of grace to assist the saints to persevere, and perseverance as necessary for final salvation. Therefore every sermon is a "salvation sermon"—not just because of its aim to convert sinners, but also in its aim to preserve the holy affections of the saints and so enable them to confirm their calling and election, and be saved.

In summary, then, when Jonathan Edwards became still and knew that God is God, the vision before his eyes was of an absolutely sovereign God, self-sufficient and all-sufficient, infinite in holiness, and therefore perfectly glorious. God's actions are never motivated to meet his deficiencies (since he has none), but are always motivated to display his sufficiency (which is infinite). He does what he does for the sake of his glory. Our duty and privilege, therefore, is to conform to this goal and reflect the value of God's glory by delighting in it. Our calling and our joy is to render visible God's glorious grace by trusting him with all our heart as long as we live.

7

Make God Supreme
The Preaching of Edwards

What sort of preaching results from Edwards's vision of God? What sort of preaching did God use to ignite the Great Awakening in New England during Edwards's ministry at Northampton? Spiritual awakening is the sovereign work of God, to be sure. But he uses means, especially preaching. "Of his own will he brought us forth *by the word of truth*" (James 1:18, emphasis added). "It pleased God *through the folly of what we preach* to save those who believe" (1 Cor. 1:21, emphasis added).

The essence of Edwards's preaching might be found in ten characteristics, which are so valuable for our own day that they will be presented as relevant challenges, and not just as facts about Edwards. These characteristics may be gleaned both from the way he preached and from his occasional comments about preaching.

Stir Up Holy Affections

Good preaching aims to stir up "holy affections"—such emotions as hatred for sin, delight in God, hope in His promises, gratitude for his mercy, desire for holiness, and tender compassion. The reason is that the absence of holy affections in Christians is odious. "The things of religion are so great, that there can be no suitableness in the exercises of our hearts, to their nature and importance, unless they be lively and powerful. In nothing is vigor in the actings of our inclinations so requisite, as in religion; and in nothing is lukewarmness so odious."[1] Elsewhere Edwards remarked, "If true religion lies much in the *affections,* we may infer, that *such a way of preaching the word* . . . as has a tendency deeply to affect the hearts of those who attend . . . is much to be desired."[2]

Of course the dignified clergy in Boston saw great danger in targeting the emotions like this. For example, Charles Chauncy charged that it was "a plain stubborn Fact, that the Passions have, generally, in these Times, been apply'd to, as though the main Thing in Religion was to throw them into Disturbance."[3] Edwards's answer was crafted and balanced:

I don't think ministers are to be blamed for raising the affections of their hearers too high, if that which they are affected with be only that which is worthy of affection, and their affections are not raised beyond a proportion to their importance. . . . I should think myself in the way of my duty to raise the affections of my hearers as high as possibly I can, provided that they are affected with nothing but truth, and with affections that are not disagreeable to the nature of what they are affected with. I know it has long been fashionable to despise a very earnest and pathetical way of preaching; and they, and they only, have been valued as preachers, that have shown the greatest extent of learning, and strength of reason, and correctness of method and language: but I humbly conceive it has been for want of understanding, or duly considering human nature, that such preaching has been thought to have the greatest tendency to answer the ends of preaching; and the experience of the present and past ages abundantly confirms the same[4]

Probably in our day someone would ask Edwards why he does not make external deeds of love and justice his goal rather than just the affections of the heart. The answer is that he does make behavior his aim, namely, by aiming to transform the spring of behavior—the affections. He chooses this strategy for two reasons. One is that a good tree can't bear bad fruit. The longest section of *A Treatise Concerning Religious Affections* is devoted to proving this thesis: "Gracious and holy affections have their exercise and fruit in Christian practice."[5] Edwards aimed at the affections because they are the springs of all godly action. Make the tree good and its fruit will be good.

The other reason Edwards aimed to stir up holy affections is that "no external fruit is good, which does not proceed from such exercises."[6] Outward acts of benevolence and piety which do not flow from the new and God-given affections of the heart, which delight to depend on God and seek his glory, are only legalism and have no value in honoring God. If you give your body to be burned and have not love it profits nothing (1 Cor. 13:3).

Therefore good preaching aims to stir up holy affections in those who hear. It targets the heart.

Enlighten the Mind

Yes, Edwards said, "Our people don't so much need to have their heads stored as to have their hearts touched and they stand in the greatest need of that sort of preaching that has the greatest tendency to do this."[7] But there is a world of difference between the way Edwards aims to move the hearts of his people and the way relational, psychologically oriented preachers today might try to move their hearers.

Edwards preached an ordination sermon in 1744 on the text about John the Baptist, "He was a burning and a shining light" (John 5:35). His main point was that a preacher must burn and shine. There must be heat in the heart and light in the mind—and no more heat than justified by the light:

> If a minister has light without heat, and entertains his auditory with learned discourses, without a savour of the power of godliness, or any appearance of fervency of spirit, and zeal for God and the good of souls, he may gratify itching ears, and fill the heads of his people with empty notions; but it will not be very likely to reach their hearts, or save their souls. And if, on the other hand, he be driven on with a fierce and intemperate zeal, and vehement heat, without light, he will be likely to kindle the like unhallowed flame in his people, and to fire their corrupt passions and affections; but will make them never the better, nor

lead them a step towards heaven, but drive them apace the other way.[8]

Heat *and* light; burning *and* shining; it is crucial to bring light to the mind because affections that do not rise from the mind's apprehension of truth are not holy affections. For example, he says, "That faith, which is without spiritual light, is not the faith of the children of the light and of the day, but the presumption of the children of darkness. And therefore to press and urge them to believe, without any spiritual light or sight, tends greatly to help forward the delusions of the prince of darkness."[9]

He speaks even more strongly when he says, "Suppose the religious affections of persons indeed arise from a strong persuasion of the truth of the Christian religion; their affections are not the better, unless it be a *reasonable* persuasion or conviction. By a reasonable conviction, I mean a conviction founded on *real evidence*, or upon that which is a good reason, or just ground of conviction."[10] So the good preacher will make it his aim to give his hearers "good reason" and "just ground" for the affections he is trying to stir up. Edwards can never be brought forward as an example of one who manipulated emotions. He treated his hearers as creatures of reason and sought to move their hearts only by giving the light of truth to the mind.

Therefore he taught that it is "very profitable for ministers in their preaching, to endeavor clearly and distinctly to explain the doctrines of religion, and unravel the difficulties that attend them, and to confirm them with strength of reason and argumentation, and also to observe some easy and clear method and order in their discourses, for the help of the understanding and memory."[11] The reason for this is that good preaching aims to enlighten the mind of the hearers with divine truth. It was a wonderful combination that God used to awaken New England 250 years ago: heat and light; burning and shining; head and heart; deep doctrine and deep delight. May not God use this means again today as we seek to enlighten the mind and inflame the heart?

Saturate with Scripture

I say that good preaching is "saturated with Scripture" and not "based on Scripture" because Scripture is more (not less) than the basis for good preaching. Preaching that proclaims God's supremacy does not begin with Scripture as a basis and then wander off to other things. It oozes Scripture.

My continual advice to beginning preachers is, "Quote the text! Quote the text! Say the actual words of the text again and again. Show the people where your ideas are coming from." Most people do not easily follow the connections a preacher sees between his words and the text. They must be shown again and again with actual quotes from Scripture. Edwards expended great energy to write out whole passages in his sermon manuscripts to support what he was saying. He quoted in full verse after verse that cast light on his theme. Edwards thought of these anchoring texts as "the beams of the light of the Sun of righteousness; they are the light by which ministers must be enlightened, and the light they are to hold forth to their hearers; and they are the fire whence their hearts and the hearts of their hearers must be enkindled."[12]

He looked back once on his early pastoral experience and recalled above other experiences his delight in Scripture study. "Oftentimes in reading it, every word seemed to touch my heart. I felt a harmony between something in my heart, and those sweet and powerful words. I seemed often to see so much light exhibited by every sentence, and such a refreshing food communicated, that I could not get along in reading; often dwelling long on one sentence, to see the wonders contained in it; yet almost every sentence seemed to be full of wonders."[13]

One has to stand in awe of Edwards's thorough knowledge of the Bible, especially since he was also conversant with the best theological, moral, and philosophical learning of his day. As a student he made this life resolution: "*Resolved,* To study the Scriptures so steadily, constantly, and frequently, as that I may find, and plainly perceive, myself to grow in the knowledge of the same."[14] "Steadily," "constantly," "frequently"—this was the source of the wealth of Scripture in Edwards's sermons.

His practice in study was to take hundreds of notes and pursue any thread of insight as far as he could. "My method of study, from my first beginning the work of the ministry, has been very much by writing; applying myself, in this way, to improve every important hint; pursuing the clue to my utmost, when anything in reading, meditation, or conversation, has been suggested to my mind, that seemed to promise light in any weighty point; thus penning what appeared to me my best thoughts, on innumerable subjects, for my own benefit."[15] His pen was his exegetical eye. Like John Calvin (who said this in the introduction to the *Institutes of the Christian Religion*), he learned as he wrote and he wrote as he learned. In what he saw by this method he makes most of our hurried meditations on Scripture look very superficial.

To read Edwards is to read the Bible through the eyes of one who understands it deeply and feels it with all his heart. His preaching was saturated with Scripture. Ours should be as well. Let us follow Edwards's counsel to "be well studied in divinity, well acquainted with the written word of God [and] mighty in the Scriptures."[16]

Employ Analogies and Images

Experience and Scripture teach that the heart is most powerfully touched, not when the mind is entertaining abstract ideas, but when it is filled with vivid images of amazing reality. Edwards was, to be sure, a metaphysician and a philosopher of the highest order. He believed in the importance of theory, but he also knew that abstractions kindled few affections, and new affections were the goal of preaching. So Edwards strained to make the glories of heaven look irresistibly beautiful and the torments of hell look intolerably horrible. Abstract theological truth came to life in common events and experiences.

Sereno Dwight says that "those who are conversant with the writings of Edwards, need not be informed that all his works, even the most metaphysical, are rich in illustration, or that his sermons abound with imagery of every kind, adapted to make a powerful and lasting impression."[17]

In his most famous sermon, "Sinners in the Hands of an Angry God," Edwards referred to the phrase, "the winepress of the fierceness and wrath of Almighty God" (Rev. 19:15 KJV). He says, "The words are exceedingly terrible. If it had only been said, 'the wrath of God,' the words would have implied that which is infinitely dreadful: but it is 'the fierceness and wrath of God.' The fury of God! The fierceness of Jehovah! O how dreadful must that be! Who can utter or conceive what such expressions carry in them?"[18]

There is Edwards's challenge to every preacher of the Word of God. Who can find images and analogies that come anywhere near creating the profound feelings we ought to have when we consider realities like hell and heaven? We dare not fault Edwards's images of hell unless we are prepared to fault the Bible. For in his own view (and I surely think he was right) he was only groping for language that might come close to what awesome realities are contained in biblical phrases like "the winepress of the fierceness and wrath of Almighty God."

Today we do just the opposite. We grope for circumlocutions of hell and create images as far from the horror of the biblical phrases as we can. Partly as a result, our attempts to make heaven look attractive and make grace look amazing often appear extremely pitiful. We would do well to labor with Edwards to find images and analogies that produce impressions in our people comparable to reality.

But it was not only heaven and hell that pushed Edwards to find analogies and images. He used the analogy of a surgeon with a scalpel to explain some kinds of preaching. He used the similarity of a human embryo to an animal embryo to show that at conversion a new life with all its new affections may be there but not yet show itself as fully distinct from the unregenerate. He pictured the pure heart with remaining impurities as a vat of fermenting liquor trying to get clean of all sediment. And he saw holiness in the soul as a garden of God with all manner of pleasant flowers. His sermons abound with images and analogies to give light to the understanding and heat to the affections.

Use Threat and Warning

Edwards did know his hell; but he knew his heaven even better. I can vividly recall the winter evenings during graduate school when my wife Noël and I sat on our couch in Munich, Germany, reading together Edwards's sermon, "Heaven Is a World of Love." What a magnificent vision! Surely if the congregation saw us preachers painting such pictures of glory and panting after God the way Edwards did, there would be a new awakening in the churches.

But those who have the largest hearts for heaven shudder most deeply at the horrors of hell. Edwards was fully persuaded that hell is real. "This doctrine is indeed awful and dreadful, yet 'tis of God."¹⁹ Therefore he esteemed the threats of Jesus as the strident tones of love. "Whoever says, 'You fool,' shall be liable to the hell of fire" (Matt. 5:22). "It is better that you lose one of your members than that your whole body go into hell" (Matt. 5:30). "Fear him who can destroy both soul and body in hell" (Matt. 10:28). Edwards could not remain silent where Jesus was so vocal. Hell awaits every unconverted person. Love must warn them with the threats of the Lord.

The use of threat or warning in preaching to the saints is rare today for at least two reasons: It produces guilt and fear, which are considered to be unproductive, and it seems theologically inappropriate because the saints are secure and don't need to be warned or threatened. Edwards rejected both reasons. When fear and guilt correspond with the true state of things it is reasonable and loving to stir them up. And the saints are only as secure as they are willing to give heed to biblical warnings and persevere in godliness. "Let him who thinks that he stands take heed lest he fall" (1 Cor. 10:12).

Edwards said that God set things up for the church in such a way "that when their love decays . . . fear should arise. They need fear then to restrain them from sin, [and] to excite them to care for the good of their souls. But God hath so ordered, that when love rises . . . then fear should vanish, and be driven away."[20]

So on the one hand, Edwards says, "God's wrath and future punishment are proposed to all sorts of men, as motives to . . . obedience, not only to the wicked, but also to the godly."[21] On the other hand, he says that holy love and hope are more efficacious to make the heart tender and to fill it with a dread of sin than is the slavish fear of hell.[22] Preaching about hell is never an end in itself. You can't frighten anyone into heaven. Heaven is for people who love purity, not for people who simply loathe pain. Nevertheless, Edwards said, "Some talk of it as an unreasonable thing to think to fright persons to heaven; but I think it is a reasonable thing to endeavor to fright persons away from hell—tis a reasonable thing to fright a person out of a house on fire."[23]

Therefore good preaching will deliver the biblical messages of warning to congregations of saints as Paul did when he said to the Galatians, "I warn you . . . that those who do such things shall not inherit the Kingdom of God" (Gal. 5:21), or when he said, "Do not be arrogant but be afraid" (Rom. 11:20 NIV). Peter added, "If you invoke as Father him who judges each one impartially according to his deeds, conduct yourselves with fear throughout the time of your exile" (1 Pet. 1:17). Such warnings are the somber tones which help good preaching to display with lavish colors the magnificent promises and pictures of heaven as Paul did when he said to the Ephesians that in the coming ages God will "show the immeasurable riches of his grace in kindness toward us in Christ Jesus" (Eph. 2:7).

Plead for a Response

Can a Calvinist such as Edwards really plead with people to flee hell and cherish heaven? Do not total depravity and unconditional election and irresistible grace make such pleading inconsistent?

Edwards learned his Calvinism from the Bible and therefore was spared many errors into which some other preachers of his day fell. He did not infer that unconditional election or irresistible grace or supernatural regeneration or the inability of the natural man led to the conclusion that the use of pleading was inappropriate. He said, "Sinners . . . should be earnestly invited to come and accept of a Savior, and yield their hearts unto him, with all the winning, encouraging arguments for them . . . that the Gospel affords."[24]

I recall hearing a preacher in the Reformed tradition several years ago preach from 1 Corinthians 16, which ends with the fearful threat, "If any one has no love for the Lord, let him be accursed" (vs. 22). He alluded to it in passing, but there was no yearning or pleading with the people to love Christ and to escape the terrible curse. I marveled that this could be. There is a tradition of hyper-Calvinism which says that God's purpose to save the elect gives preachers warrant to invite to Christ only those who give evidence that they are already quickened and drawn by the Spirit. It breeds a kind of preaching that informs but does not plead with sinners to repent. Edwards, as Charles Spurgeon after him, knew that this was not authentic Calvinism; it was contrary to Scripture and unworthy of the Reformed tradition.

In fact, Edwards wrote *The Freedom of the Will* to show that "God's moral government over mankind, His treating them as moral agents, making them the objects of His commands, counsels, calls, warnings, expostulations, promises, threatenings, rewards and punishments, is not inconsistent with a determining disposal of all events, of every kind, throughout the universe."[25] In other words, pleading with our listeners to make a response to our preaching is not at odds with a high doctrine of the sovereignty of God.

When we preach, to be sure, it is *God* who affects the results for which we long. But that does not rule out earnest appeals for our people to respond. For as Edwards explains,

> We are not merely passive, nor yet does God do some, and we do the rest. But God does all, and we do all. God produces all, and we act all. For that is what he produces, *viz.* our own acts. God is the only proper author and fountain; we only are the proper actors. We are, in different respects, wholly passive and wholly active.
>
> In the Scriptures the same things are represented as from God and from us. God is said to convert [2 Tim. 2:25], and men are said to convert and turn [Acts 2:38]. God makes a new heart [Ezek. 36:26], and we are commanded to make us a new heart [Ezek. 18:31]. God circumcises the heart [Deut. 30:6], and we are commanded to circumcise our own hearts [Deut.

10:16] . . . These things are agreeable to that text, "God worketh in you both to will and to do [Phil. 2:13]."[26]

Therefore Edwards pled with his people to respond to the Word of God and be saved. "Now, if you have any sort of prudence for your own salvation, and have not a mind to go to hell, improve this season! Now is the accepted time! Now is the day of salvation . . . Do not harden your hearts at such a day as this!"[27] Almost every sermon has a long section called "Application," where Edwards screws in the implications of his doctrine and presses for a response. He did not give what is known today as an "altar call," but he did "call" and expostulate and plead for his people to respond to God.

So it seems that God has been pleased to give awakening power to preaching which does not shrink back from the loving threatenings of the Lord, and which lavishes the saints with incomparable promises of grace, and which pleads passionately and lovingly that no one hear the Word of God in vain. It is a tragedy to see pastors state the facts and sit down. Good preaching pleads with people to respond to the Word of God.

Probe the Workings of the Heart

Powerful preaching is like surgery. Under the anointing of the Holy Spirit, it locates, lances, and removes the infection of sin. Sereno Dwight, one of Edwards's early biographers, said of him, "His knowledge of the human heart, and its operations, has scarcely been equalled by that of any uninspired preacher."28 My own experience as a patient on Edwards's operating table confirms this judgment.

Edwards did not get such a profound knowledge of the human soul from hobnobbing with the Northampton parishioners. Dwight said that he had never known of any man more constantly retired from the world to give himself to reading and contemplations. It may have begun with a typical Puritan bent toward introspection. On July 30, 1723, when he was nineteen years old, Edwards wrote in his diary, "Have concluded to endeavor to work myself into duties by searching and tracing back all the real reasons why I do them not, and narrowly searching out all the subtle subterfuges of my thoughts."29 A week later he wrote, "Very much convinced of the extraordinary deceitfulness of the heart, and how exceedingly . . . appetite blinds the mind, and brings it into entire subjection."30 So Dwight is certainly right when he says that much of Edwards's insight into the human heart came "from his thorough acquaintance with his own heart."31

A second thing that gave Edwards such a profound insight into the workings of the heart was the necessity of sorting out the wheat and the chaff in the intense religious experiences of his people during the Great Awakening. *Treatise Concerning Religious Affections,* which he had originally preached as sermons in 1742 and 1743, is a devastating exposure of self-deception in religion. It probes relentlessly to the root of our depravity. This kind of sustained and careful examination of the religious experiences of his people gave Edwards a remarkable grasp of the workings of their hearts.

A third cause of Edwards's knowledge of the human heart was his extraordinary insight into God's testimony about it in Scripture. For example, he notices in Galatians 4:15 that the religious experience of the Galatians had been so intense that they would have plucked out their eyes for him. But then Edwards notices also in verse 11 of that chapter that Paul says he might have "labored over you in vain." From this Edwards infers shrewdly that the height or intensity of religious affections (readiness to pluck out the eye) is no sure sign that they are genuine (since his labor might have been in vain).[32] Years and years of this kind of study make for a profound surgeon of souls. It produces a preaching that uncovers the secret things of the heart. And more than once it has led to a great awakening in the church.

Edwards said that every minister of the Word "must be acquainted with experimental religion, and not ignorant of the inward operations of the Spirit of God, nor of Satan's devices."[33] Again and again when I read Edwards's sermons I have the profound experience of having myself laid bare. The secrets of my heart are plowed up. The deceitful workings of my heart are exposed. The potential beauty of new affections appears attractive. I find that they are even taking root as I read.

Edwards again compared the preacher to a surgeon: "To blame a minister for declaring the truth to those who are under awakenings, and not immediately administering comfort to them, is like blaming a surgeon because when he has begun to thrust in his lance, whereby he has already put his patient to great pain . . . he won't stay his hand, but goes on to thrust it in further, till he comes to the core of the wound. Such a compassionate physician, who as soon as his patient began to flinch, should withdraw his hand . . . would be one that would heal the hurt slightly, crying, 'Peace, peace, when there is no peace.'"[34] This analogy of the surgeon and the scalpel is indeed apt for his own preaching. We don't want to lie naked on the table, and we don't want to be cut, but oh, the joy of having the cancer out! Therefore good preaching, like good surgery, probes the workings of the human heart.

Yield to the Holy Spirit in Prayer

In 1735 Edwards preached a sermon, "The Most High, a Prayer Hearing God." In it he said, "God has been pleased to constitute prayer to be antecedent to the bestowment of mercy; and he is pleased to bestow mercy in consequence of prayer, as though he were prevailed on by prayer."[35] The goal of preaching is utterly dependent on the mercy of God for its fulfillment. Therefore, the preacher must labor to put his preaching under divine influence by prayer.

By this means the Holy Spirit assists the preacher. But Edwards didn't believe the assistance came in the form of words being immediately suggested to the mind. If that's all the Spirit did a preacher could be a devil and do his work. No, the Holy Spirit fills the heart with holy affections and the heart fills the mouth. "When a person is in an holy and lively frame in secret prayer, it will wonderfully supply him with matter and with expressions . . . [in] preaching."[36]

Edwards counsels the young ministers of his day that they, "in order to be burning and shining lights, should walk closely with God, and keep near to Christ; that they may ever be enlightened and enkindled by him. And they should be much in seeking God, and conversing with him by prayer, who is the fountain of light and love."[37]

Early in his own ministry, he said, "I spent most of my time in thinking of divine things, year after year; often walking alone in the woods, and solitary places, for meditation, soliloquy, and prayer, and converse with God; and it was always my manner, at such times, to sing forth my contemplations. I was almost constantly in ejaculatory prayer, wherever I was. Prayer seemed to be natural to me, as the breath by which the inward burnings of my heart had vent."[38]

Besides private prayer Edwards threw himself into the wider prayer movement of his day that was spreading from Scotland. He wrote one work with the descriptive title, *An Humble Attempt to Promote Explicit Agreement and Visible Union of God's People in Extraordinary Prayer for the Revival of Religion and Advancement of Christ's Kingdom on Earth.*[39] The secret prayer of the preacher and the concerts of prayer among the people conspire in the mercy of God to bring down the demonstration of the Spirit and of power.

Good preaching is born of good praying. And it will come forth with the power that caused the Great Awakening when it is delivered under the mighty prayer-wrought influence of the Holy Spirit.

Be Broken and Tenderhearted

Good preaching comes from a spirit of brokenness and tenderness. For all his authority and power Jesus was attractive because he was "gentle and lowly in heart" which made him a place of rest (Matt. 11:28–29). "When he saw the multitudes, he was moved with compassion on them, because they fainted, and were scattered abroad, as sheep having no shepherd" (Matt. 9:36 KJV). There is, in the Spirit-filled preacher, a tender affection that sweetens every promise and softens with tears every warning and rebuke. "We were gentle among you, even as a nurse cherisheth her children. So being affectionately desirous of you, we were willing to have imparted unto you not the gospel of God only, but also our own souls, because ye were dear unto us" (1 Thess. 2:7–8 KJV).

One of the secrets of Edwards's power in the pulpit was the "brokenhearted" tenderness with which he could address the weightiest matters. We catch the scent of this demeanor in his own words: "All gracious affections . . . are brokenhearted affections. A truly Christian love . . . is a humble brokenhearted love. The desires of the saints, however earnest, are humble desires: their hope is an humble hope; and their joy, even when it is unspeakable, and full of glory, is an humble, brokenhearted joy, and leaves the Christian more poor in spirit, and more like a little child and more disposed to an universal lowliness of behavior."[40]

Genuine spiritual power in the pulpit is not synonymous with loudness. Hard hearts are not likely to be broken by shrill voices. Edwards was persuaded from Scripture that "gracious affections do not tend to make men bold, forward, noisy, and boisterous; but rather to speak trembling."[41] The eye of divine blessing is upon the meek and trembling: "This is the man to whom I will look [says the Lord], he that is humble and contrite in spirit, and trembles at my word" (Isa. 66:2).

Therefore, Edwards says that ministers should cultivate the quiet, lamb-like spirit of Christ, "the same spirit of forgiveness of injuries; the same spirit of charity, of fervent love and extensive benevolence; the same disposition to pity the miserable, to weep with those that weep, to help men under their calamities of both soul and body, to hear and grant the requests of the needy, and relieve the afflicted; the same spirit of condescension to the poor and mean, tenderness and gentleness towards the weak, and great and effectual love to enemies."[42]

The spirit we long to see in people must be in ourselves first. That will never happen until, as Edwards says, we know our own emptiness and helplessness and terrible sinfulness. Edwards lived in a kind of spiralling oscillation between humiliation for his sin and exultation in his Savior. He describes his experience like this: "Often since I lived in this town, I have had very affecting views of my own sinfulness and vileness; very frequently to such a degree as to hold me in a kind of loud weeping, sometimes for a considerable time together; so that I have often been forced to shut myself up."[43] It is not hard to imagine the depth of earnestness that this kind of experience brought to the preaching of God's Word.

But of course one is on the precipice of despair when one focuses only on sin. This was not Edwards's aim nor his experience. His response to guilt made it an intensely evangelical and liberating experience: "I love to think of coming to Christ, to receive salvation of him, poor in spirit, and quite empty of self, humbly exalting him alone; cut off entirely from my own root, in order to grow into, and out of Christ; to have God in Christ be my all in all."[44] This is the supremacy of God in the life of the preacher that leads straight to God's supremacy in preaching.

Plainly Edwards's intensity was not a harsh and loud and belligerent thing. Edwards's power was not in rhetorical flourish, or ear-splitting thunders. It was born in brokenhearted affections.

Edwards was described by Thomas Prince as "a preacher of a low and moderate voice, a natural way of delivery; and without any agitation of body, or anything else in the manner to excite attention; except his habitual and great solemnity, looking and speaking as in the presence of God."[45] He stands as a rare testimony to the truth that preaching that makes God supreme comes from a spirit of brokenness and tenderness.

Be Intense

Compelling preaching gives the impression that something very great is at stake. With Edwards's view of the reality of heaven and hell and the necessity of persevering in a life of holy affections and godliness, eternity was at stake every Sunday. This sets him apart from the average preacher today. Our emotional rejection of hell, and our facile view of conversion and the abundant false security we purvey have created an atmosphere in which the great biblical intensity of preaching is almost impossible.

Edwards so believed in the realities of which he spoke, and so longed for their reality to stagger his people, that when George Whitefield preached these realities with power in Edwards's pulpit, Edwards wept during the whole service. Edwards could no more imagine speaking in a cold or casual or indifferent or flippant manner about the great things of God than he could imagine a father discussing coolly the collapse of a flaming house upon his children (see pp. 48–49).

Lack of intensity in preaching can only communicate that the preacher does not believe or has never been seriously gripped by the reality of which he speaks—or that the subject matter is insignificant. This was never the case with Edwards. He stood in continual awe at the weight of the truth he was charged to proclaim.

One contemporary said that Edwards's eloquence was "the power of presenting an important truth before an audience, with overwhelming weight of argument, and with such intenseness of feeling, that the whole soul of the speaker is thrown into every part of the conception and delivery; so that the solemn attention of the whole audience is riveted, from the beginning to the close, and impressions are left that cannot be effaced."[46]

In his introduction to John Gillies's *Historical Collections of Accounts of Revival*, Horatius Bonar in 1845 described the kind of preachers God had been pleased to use to awaken his church through the centuries:

> They felt their infinite responsibility as stewards of the mysteries of God and shepherds appointed by the Chief Shepherd to gather in and watch over souls. They lived and labored and preached like men on whose lips the immortality of thousands hung. Everything they did and spoke bore the stamp of earnestness, and proclaimed to all with whom they came into contact that the matters about which they had been sent to treat were of infinite moment. . . . Their preaching seems to have been of the most masculine and fearless kind, falling on the audience with tremendous power. It was not vehement, it was not fierce, it was not noisy; it was far too solemn to be such; it was massive, weighty, cutting, piercing, sharper than a two-edged sword.[47]

So it was with Jonathan Edwards just 250 years ago. By precept and example Edwards calls us to "an exceeding affectionate way of preaching about the great things of religion" and to flee from a "moderate, dull indifferent way of speaking."[48] We simply must signify, without melodrama or affectation, that the reality behind our message is breathtaking.

Of course that assumes that we have seen the God of Jonathan Edwards. If we don't share the greatness of his vision of God we will not approach the greatness of his preaching. On the other hand, if God in his grace should see fit to open our eyes to the vision of Edwards, if we were granted to taste the sweet sovereignty of the Almighty the way Edwards tasted it, then a renewal of the pulpit in our day would be possible—indeed inevitable.

Conclusion

People are starving for the grandeur of God, and the vast majority do not know it. Those who do say, "O God, thou art my God, I seek thee, my soul thirsts for thee; my flesh faints for thee, as in a dry and weary land where no water is" (Ps. 63:1). But most do not discern that they were made to thrill at the panorama of God's power and glory. They seek to fill the void in other ways. And even those who go to church—how many of them can say when they leave, "I have looked upon thee in the sanctuary, beholding thy power and glory" (Ps. 63:2)?

The glory of God is of infinite worth. It is the heart of what the apostles preached: "the light of the knowledge of the glory of God in the face of Christ" (2 Cor. 4:6). It is the goal of every Christian act: "Whatever you do, do all to the glory of God" (1 Cor. 10:31). It is the focus of all Christian hope: "We rejoice in hope of the glory of God" (Rom. 5:2). It will some day replace the sun and moon as the light of life: "The city has no need of sun or moon to shine upon it, for the glory of God is its light" (Rev. 21:23). And even now, before that great day, "the heavens are telling the glory of God" (Ps. 19:1). When people discover the worth of God's glory—when God says, "Let there be light," and opens the eyes of the blind—they are like people who find a treasure hidden in a field and, full of joy, sell all they have to buy that field. They are like Moses, who cried to the Lord, "I pray thee, show me thy glory" (Exod. 33:18).

This is the heart-pang of every human being. Only a few know it. Only a few diagnose the longing beneath every human desire—the longing to see God. If only people could articulate the silent cry of their hearts, would they not say, "One thing have I asked of the LORD, that will I seek after . . . to behold the beauty of the LORD . . ." (Ps. 27:4)? But, instead, the truth is held down in unrighteousness, and people do not see fit to have God in their knowledge, and even many who name the God of Israel have "changed their glory for that which does not profit" (Rom. 1:18, 28; Jer. 2:11).

Christian preachers, more than all others, should know that people are starving for God. If anyone in all the world should be able to say, "I have looked upon thee in the sanctuary, beholding thy power and glory," it is the herald of God. Who but preachers will look out over the wasteland of secular culture and say, "Behold your God!"? Who will tell the people that God is great and greatly to be praised? Who will paint for them the landscape of God's grandeur? Who will remind them with tales of wonder that God has triumphed over every foe? Who will cry out above every crisis, "Your God reigns!"? Who will labor to find words that can carry the "gospel of the glory of the blessed God"?

If God is not supreme in our preaching, where in this world will the people hear about the supremacy of God? If we do not spread a banquet of God's beauty on Sunday morning, will not our people seek in vain to satisfy their inconsolable longing with the cotton candy pleasures of pastimes and religious hype? If the fountain of living water does not flow from the mountain of God's sovereign grace on Sunday morning, will not the people hew for themselves cisterns on Monday, broken cisterns that can hold no water (Jer. 2:13)?

We are called to be "stewards of the mysteries of God" (1 Cor. 4:1). And the great mystery is "Christ in you the hope of glory" (Col. 1:27). And that glory is the glory of God. And "it is required of stewards that they be found faithful"—faithful in magnifying the supreme glory of the one eternal God, not magnifying as a microscope that makes small things look bigger; but as a telescope that makes unimaginably great galaxies of glory visible to the human eye.

If we love our people, if we love the "other sheep" that are not yet gathered into the fold, if we love the fulfillment of God's global purpose, we will labor to "spread a table in the wilderness." People everywhere are starving for the enjoyment of God. For, as Jonathan Edwards said, "The enjoyment of God is the only happiness with which our souls can be satisfied.

To go to heaven, fully to enjoy God, is infinitely better than the most pleasant accommodations here. Fathers and mothers, husbands, wives, or children, or the company of earthly friends, are but shadows; but God is the substance. These are but scattered beams, but God is the sun. These are but streams. But God is the ocean."[1]

Endnotes

Preface

1. Andrew Bonar, ed., *Memoir and Remains of Robert Murray McCheyne* (repr. ed., Grand Rapids: Baker Book House, 1978), 258.

2. Mark Noll, "Jonathan Edwards, Moral Philosophy, and the Secularization of American Christian Thought," *Reformed Journal* (February 1983): 26. Emphasis author's.

3. Charles Colson, "Introduction," in Jonathan Edwards, *Religious Affections*, (Portland: Multnomah, 1984), xxiii, xxxiv.

4. Iain Murray, *The Forgotten Spurgeon* (Edinburgh: Banner of Truth, 1966), 36.

The Goal of Preaching

1. Charles H. Spurgeon, *Lectures to My Students* (Grand Rapids: Zondervan, 1972), 26.

2. James Stewart, *Heralds of God* (Grand Rapids: Baker Book House, 1972), 73. This quote comes from William Temple, who formulated it to define worship, but Stewart borrowed it as giving "precisely the aims and ends of preaching.

3. John H. Jowett, *The Preacher: His Life and Work* (New York: Harper, 1912), 96, 98.

4. Spurgeon, *Lectures*, 146.

5. Samuel Johnson, *Lives of the English Poets* (London: Oxford University Press), 2:365.

6. Christopher Catherwood, *Five Evangelical Leaders* (Wheaton: Harold Shaw, 1985), 170.

7. Cotton Mather, *Student and Preacher, or Directions for a Candidate of the Ministry* (London: Hindmarsh, 1726), v.

8. An extended exegetical defense of this statement is given in Appendix 1 of John Piper, *Desiring God* (Portland: Multnomah, 1986).

9. This is the thesis of *Desiring God,* where its implications for areas of life other than preaching are developed.

The Ground of Preaching

1. For a defense and exposition of this definition see John Piper, *The Justification of God* (Grand Rapids: Baker Book House, 1983).

The Gift of Preaching

1. Phillips Brooks, *Lectures on Preaching* (Grand Rapids: Baker Book House, 1969), 106.

2. Of course the vast majority of the people of the world are not literate. The most urgent missionary preaching will not be the same form of preaching as is needed in most of the pulpits of America where Christians sit with Bibles in hand. Nevertheless, I want to make a case that even preaching to nonliterate peoples should include quoting much Scripture from memory and making clear that the authority of the preacher comes from an inspired book. Doing expository preaching for nonliterate cultures is a challenge that needs much attention.

3. Quoted in John R. W. Stott, *Between Two Worlds* (Grand Rapids: Eerdmans, 1982), 32.

4. Sereno Dwight, *Memoirs,* in S. Dwight, ed., *The Works of Jonathan Edwards,* (1834; repr. ed., Edinburgh: Banner of Truth, 1974), 1:xxi. Hereafter edition cited as *Banner.*

5. Quoted in Murray, *Forgotten Spurgeon,* 34.

The Gravity and Gladness of Preaching

1. Jonathan Edwards, "The True Excellency of a Gospel Minister," *Banner,* 2:958.

2. Jonathan Edwards, *The Great Awakening,* ed. C. Goen, *The Works of Jonathan Edwards* (New Haven: Yale University Press, 1972), 4:272. Hereafter edition cited as *Yale.*

3. Dwight, *Memoirs,* in *Banner,* 1:clxxxix.

4. Ibid., 1:cxc.

5. Stewart, *Heralds of God,* 102.

6. Andrew W. Blackwood, ed., *The Protestant Pulpit* (Grand Rapids: Baker Book House, 1977), 311.

7. James W. Alexander, *Thoughts on Preaching* (Edinburgh: Banner of Truth, 1975), 264.

8. Brooks, *Lectures,* 82–83.

9. Jonathan Edwards, *Religious Affections*, ed. John E. Smith, in *Yale* (1959), 2:339.

10. Quoted in Stott, *Between Two Worlds*, 325.

11. John H. Jowett, *The Preacher: His Life and Work* (New York: Harper, 1912), 89.

12. Bennet Tyler and Andrew Bonar, *The Life and Labors of Asahel Nettleton* (Edinburgh: Banner of Truth, 1975), 65, 67, 80.

13. William Sprague, *Lectures on Revivals of Religion* (London: Banner of Truth, 1959), 119–20. The rest of this passage, though not included here, is equally powerful.

14. Quoted in Murray, *Forgotten Spurgeon*, 38.

15. Spurgeon, *Lectures*, 212.

16. Quoted in Stewart, *Heralds of God*, 207.

17. Quoted in Charles Bridges, *The Christian Ministry* (Edinburgh: Banner of Truth, 1967), 214.

18. B. B. Warfield, "The Religious Life of Theological Students," in Mark Noll, ed., *The Princeton Theology* (Grand Rapids: Baker Book House, 1983), 263.

19. Bridges, *Christian Ministry*, 214.

20. Dwight, *Memoirs*, in *Banner*, 1: xx, xxii.

Keep God Central

1. Dwight, *Memoirs*, in *Banner*, 1: xxxix.

2. Ibid., 1:xxxviii.

3. Ibid., 1:xx.

4. Ibid., 1:xxxvi.

5. Ibid.

6. Elisabeth Dodds, *Marriage to a Difficult Man: The "Uncommon Union" of Jonathan and Sarah Edwards* (Philadelphia: Westminster, 1971), 22.

7. Jonathan Edwards: *Selections*, eds., C. H. Faust and T. Johnson (New York: Hill and Wang, 1935), 69. Hereafter cited as *Selections*.

8. Edwards, *Memoirs*, in *Banner*, 1:clxxiv–clxxv.

9. Ibid., 1:clxxvii.

10. Ibid., 1:clxxix.

Submit to Sweet Sovereignty

1. Jonathan Edwards, "The Sole Consideration, that God is God, Sufficient to Still All Objections to his Sovereignty," in *Banner*, 2:107. Emphasis Edwards's.

2. Ibid., 2:107–8.

3. Jonathan Edwards, *A Treatise Concerning Religious Affections*, in *Banner*, 1:279.

4. *Selections*, 59, 67.

5. *Banner*, 1:94–121.

6. Edwards, *Religious Affections*, in *Banner*, 1:237.

7. Ibid., 1:243.

8. Jonathan Edwards, *Miscellaneous Remarks Concerning Satisfaction for Sin*, in *Banner*, 2:569.

9. Jonathan Edwards, *Miscellaneous Remarks Concerning Faith*, in *Banner*, 2:588.

10. Ibid., 2:578–95. These observations and many similar reasonings are spread throughout Edwards's remarks in this section.

11. Jonathan Edwards, *Miscellaneous Remarks Concerning Efficacious Grace*, in *Banner*, 2:548.

12. Jonathan Edwards, *Miscellaneous Remarks Concerning Perseverance of the Saints*, in *Banner*, 2:596.

Make God Supreme

1. Edwards, *Religious Affections*, in *Banner*, 1:238.

2. Ibid., 1:244. Emphasis added.

3. Edwards, *Selections*, xx.

4. Jonathan Edwards, *Some Thoughts Concerning the Revival*, in *Yale* 4:387; see also 4:399.

5. Edwards, *Religious Affections*, in *Banner*, 1:314.

6. Ibid., 1:243.

7. Edwards, *Concerning the Revival*, in *Yale*, 4:388.

8. Edwards, "True Excellency," in *Banner*, 2:958.

9. Edwards, *Religious Affections*, in *Banner*, 1:258.

10. Ibid., 1:289. Emphasis Edwards's.

11. Edwards, *Concerning the Revival*, in *Yale*, 4:386.

12. Edwards, "True Excellency" in *Banner*, 2:959.

13. Jonathan Edwards, "Personal Narrative," *Selections*, 65.

14. Dwight, *Memoirs*, in *Banner*, 1:xxi.

15. Ibid., 1:clxxiv.

16. Edwards, "True Excellency," in *Banner*, 2:957.

17. Dwight, *Memoirs*, in *Banner*, 1:clxxxviii.

18. Jonathan Edwards, "Sinners in the Hands of an Angry God," in *Banner*, 2:10.

19. Quoted in John Gerstner, *Jonathan Edwards on Heaven and Hell* (Grand Rapids: Baker Book House, 1980), 44. This volume gives an excellent introduction to Edwards's balanced insights on the glories of heaven and the horrors of hell.

20. Edwards, *Religious Affections*, in *Banner*, 1:259. Emphasis Edwards's.

21. Edwards, *Perseverance*, in *Banner*, 2:596.

22. Edwards, *Religious Affections*, in *Banner*, 1:308.

23. Jonathan Edwards, *The Distinguishing Marks of a Work of the Spirit of God*, in *Yale*, 4:248.

24. Edwards, *Concerning the Revival*, in *Yale*, 4:391.

25. Jonathan Edwards, *Freedom of the Will*, in *Banner*, 1:87.

26. Edwards, *Efficacious Grace*, in *Banner*, 2:557.

27. Jonathan Edwards, "Pressing into the Kingdom," in *Banner*, 1:659.

28. Dwight, *Memoirs*, in *Banner*, 1:clxxxix.

29. Ibid., 1:xxx.

30. Ibid.

31. Ibid., 1:clxxxix.

32. Edwards, *Religious Affections*, in *Banner*, 1:246.

33. Edwards, "True Excellency," in *Banner*, 2:957.

34. Edwards, *Concerning the Revival*, in *Yale*, 4:390–91.

35. Jonathan Edwards, "The Most High, A Prayer-Hearing God," in *Banner*, 2:116.

36. Edwards, *Concerning the Revival*, in *Yale*, 4:438.

37. Edwards, "True Excellency," in *Banner*, 2:960.

38. Edwards, "Personal Narrative," in *Selections*, 61.

39. Edwards, *An Humble Attempt*, in *Banner*, 2:278–312.

40. Edwards, *Religious Affections*, in *Banner*, 1:302.

41. Ibid., 1:308.

42. Jonathan Edwards, "Christ the Example of Ministers," in *Banner*, 2:961.

43. Edwards, "Personal Narrative," 69.

44. Ibid., 67.

45. Quoted in *Yale*, 4:72.

46. Dwight, *Memoirs*, in *Banner*, 1:cxc.

47. Horatius Bonar, "Preface," in John Gillies, *Historical Collections of Accounts of Revival*, (1845, repr. ed., Edinburgh: Banner of Truth, 1981), vi.

48. Edwards, *Concerning the Revival*, in *Yale*, 4:386.

Conclusion

1. Jonathan Edwards, "The Christian Pilgrim," in *Banner*, 2:244.

Index of Subjects